Channel Island Plant Lore

BY
BRIAN BONNARD

The Jersey Giant Cabbage
from
"The Farmer's Magazine", 1836

Cover illustration: Duckweed from Gerard's Herbal

For Jean with Love

© Brian Bonnard

All rights reserved. No part of this publication may be reproduced, stored in a retrieval system, or transmitted, in any form or by any means, electronic, mechanical, photocopying, recording or otherwise, without the prior permission of Brian Bonnard

First published 1993

Made and printed in Great Britain by
The Guernsey Press Co. Ltd, Guernsey, Channel Islands.

ISBN 0-902550-52-7

CONTENTS

Introduction   Page 2

The Guernsey Physic Garden   Page 4

Domestic and Medicinal Uses of Plants   Page 10

Beliefs about the Properties of Plants   Page 40

Customs Involving Plants   Page 43

Magic Uses and Love Charms   Page 51

Local Sayings about Plants   Page 54

Local Island Names for Plants   Page 55

Bibliography   Page 65

Index   Page 67

History of Author

Brian Bonnard was born in 1930, trained as a botanist, worked 21 years for a pharmaceutical company, took early retirement to run the family farm, raising beef cattle. He moved to Guernsey in 1981 and immediately joined Société Guernesiaise, becoming an active member of the Botanical and Conservation sections and serving on its Council. He started a project to photograph the entire flora of the Channel Islands and write a book on it. Text is complete and he has now photographed just on 90% of the extant plants. Still awaiting a publisher as those approached all want large sponsorship money to do a book with 1,000 colour photos.

He moved to Alderney in 1986. Published *Flora of Alderney* in 1988 and also became interested in local history. Many articles published on Natural History and local history in local journals, magazines and newspapers. Published works on local history; *The Island of Dread in the Channel; Alderney in Old Photographs,* 1991, *Alderney at War; Wrecked around Alderney; Alderney in Old Photographs; a Second Series,* 1993.

CHANNEL ISLAND PLANT LORE

INTRODUCTION

The principal islands of Jersey, Guernsey, Alderney, and Sark, each have a common nucleus of plant lore and legend, with some variation in customs between them. The several variations of the ancient Norman-French language formerly spoken in the separate islands, and indeed between parishes in the two larger islands, are still in use by a small section of the population in Jersey, Guernsey and Sark. The names of common plants in these languages have in many cases been recorded and thus preserved. In Alderney where it was already much reduced since the 1800s through the influence of British garrisons, the local dialect finally died out with the almost total evacuation of the population in 1940, and virtually no written records of it exist.

The plant names are sometimes, but not always, directly related to the modern French name for the plant and are often at total variance with any translation of the English common name, perhaps instead describing their appearance, or local use. The names often show a considerable variation between the islands. The same name is sometimes used for more than one plant, or there may be several similar names with different spelling for the same plant, due to differences in pronunciation between the islands or even between parishes within the islands. Plants commonly used for domestic or medicinal purposes, as love charms, or to ward off evil, figure large in these lists, and others have given their names to areas or fields where they grow, or used to grow, or to houses or roads built on these sites.

There was a general belief in the islands that swearing at young plants, especially as they were being planted out, encouraged them to grow. Naturally many of the herbal uses, and old folk-remedies will be found to be similar to those current in Britain at the same period. Where this is so, it has not been recorded specifically, but some few may be unique to the islands. Many of the local customs involving plants however, are unique in the British Isles.

The local dialects of Norman-French are characterised by a greater number of vowels in many words compared with modern French, and rather more use of accents. They also bear some resemblance to the Breton and Welsh tongue. Where relevant (or where known), the local name for the plant is given, followed by (J), (G) or (A), for the old common names in Jersey, Guernsey or Alderney. The customs (as well as the names) sometimes varied between the islands and where they are, or were, only relevant to one island, that is indicated by its initial letter in brackets.

1. Place or house names associated with trees;

Chêne, Chesnaye, Quesnée, Chênoterie, Quenanet, etc. (Oak); *Housse*, (Holly); *Epine, Epinel, Epinette* (Thorn, white or black); *Frêne, Frênaie, Fresnaie, Frainetière*, (Ash); *Pomare, Poumarye, Pommeraie* (Orchard) (J), and *Hougue* (Mound) (G) or *Vaû* (Valley or a field) (A) *de(s) Pommier* (Apples); *Saule, Saou, Seue, Souis, Sow, Saus, or Sud* (all in A), *Saudrée, La Saulcerie* (G), some of these plus, *Sault, Scaulx, Sceaux, Saulsée, Ozier, Aubiaux*, (J), (Willow); *Ormiaux, Orme, Hormel, Ormette*, (Elms); *Codrey or Codret* (Hazel) (J); *Pêcherie*, (Peaches); *Noyer*, (Walnut); *Figuier*, (Fig); *If* (Yew); *Seuc, Seux, Seucq*, (Elder);

2. Field names associated with wild plants or crops.
(Some have now become street names as former agricultural land was built on);

Jaonnets, Jaonette, Jannières, Jeanette, Geonnais, Geon, Jan, Jon, etc, (Furzeland, all probably derived from jaune meaning yellow); *Genest, Genestel, Genestière* (J), *Genêts* (A), *Genêtes, Géniats*, (G) (to describe broom or heather land); *Mouriaux* (A) *Môre, Ronce, Ronche, Ronceraie* (J), (rough pasture, the word being derived from Blackberry bushes); *Chardons, Cardaons* (G), *Jardon, Querdron, Chardonnerie* (J) (thistles); *Hannière, Honnière* (G), *Hanniêthes, Hanière, Handois, Hane* (J), (used for places where either sedge or rush were grown); *Càmp à Suffraon* (G), (Saffron field), *Safran* (J); *Flaquée*, (G) (Reed bed); *Courtil* (enclosed field) *des Mecques* (Màcque, Ragwort) (G); *Fouailles, Fouâle* (G), *Feûgiéthe, Fougère* (J), (Bracken); *Les Quennevais* and field names *Chanvre, Cannevière, Canibut* (J) from *cannaviêthe*, places where Hemp was grown; *Lin, Linière, Lignerie* (Flax); *Panée, Panais* (J), (Parsnip); *Blé* (Corn); *Orge* (Barley); *Avoine* (Oats); *Formenteril* (Wheat); *Trémais* (Spring wheat); *Houblonerie* (Hop).

WARNING: The reader should be aware that current medical and herbal practice does not favour the use of some of the plants (or other remedies) mentioned in this work for the treatment of patients. Particular care should be exercised with the dosage of others. If you are in any doubt please consult your physician before attempting to take, or apply externally, any of the old remedies with which you are not familiar.

1. The Guernsey Physic Garden

The Romans were great herbalists, often placing much more reliance on herbalists than on doctors. As their empire expanded they took their herbs with them, and cultivated them wherever they settled. Many of the herbs in use today, both for medicinal, and for culinary use, are of southern European origin, were brought to Northern Europe and Britain during their occupation, and have now become naturalised.

Some of these undoubtedly reached the Channel Islands through the agency of the monks of the Cordeliers who set up religious house throughout the islands in the 6th-7th centuries.

The Guernsey Physic Garden of Nine Healing Herbs seems to have its origins from mediaeval times and, by Elizabethan times, was a small carefully tended plot in most countrymen's gardens there from which the housewives, and white witches, produced their simples. It was separate and distinct from the area used for culinary herbs, although some of them do have culinary uses as well.

Nine is a number of occult mystic or magic significance and in ancient times signified truth. It was believed to be under the control of the planet Saturn and 3 rows of 3 form the simplest magic square. It is used in many forms, and considered a lucky number. The remedies are more effective if the plants are grown in this form. When they were planted the herbs had to be showered with oaths in order to increase their potency and ward off evil. Men used their full repertoire, whilst ladies more frequently confined themselves to *gâche-à-pànne*, (well, goodness gracious), or *daumme-di-ti*, (well I never).

The nine herbs forming the Guernsey garden are;
Hellebore, Lavender, Rosemary, Sage, Rue, Comfrey, Wormwood, Marjoram and Vervain.

Hellebore

Black, Green and Stinking Hellebore are members of the buttercup family, and are herbaceous perennials. All parts of the plants are poisonous within the generally accepted meaning of that term, and all have similar uses and traditional names, *Setter-wort* and *Bear's-foot* being the common ones.

Black Hellebore, the familiar Christmas Rose, *la poumillière or la Rose dé Noué* (Noel) in the local patois, is so called because its roots are black. It is native to the Appennine and Pyrenees Mountains. It was believed by the ancient Egyptians and Greeks to be of value in treating mental illness. Melampos, a 2nd Century BC soothsayer, offered to cure the three daughters of the King of Argos of their mental affliction in exchange for one third of his kingdom. The King refused, and the girls got worse, one of them dying mad. The king agreed to the original terms, but Melampos increased his demand to another third of the kingdom for his brother. The king finally agreed, and the two surviving daughters were cured by Black Hellebore, and married the two brothers, at least keeping the kingdom in the family !!

Stinking and Green Hellebores are thought to be native to Britain and flower in the spring.

The fourth plant is this group is actually a lily, but with similar medicinal properties. **White False Helleborine**, has white roots. It is also probably native, and flowers in June.

Their old common names were *Neesing root, Neesewort,* and *Lingwort.*

1 Helleboras niger verus.
The true blacke Hellebor.

1 Lavandula flore caruleo.
Common Lauander.

Lavender

This shrubby native of Southern Europe was called by the Elizabethan Herbalist John Gerard, 'Lavender Spike', to distinguish it from French Lavender. Everyone is familiar with its appearance. It is evergreen, and it usually flowers in June/July. Seeds are rarely fertile, and it is usually propagated by easily rooted cuttings. The patois name for the plant is *énne touffe dé casidounne* and there is a local saying "*La casidounne tout ma détrône,* Lavender heals all". It was believed to prolong life.

Rosemary

Also a shrubby, evergreen, Southern European plant which flowers in the spring, and again at the end of the summer. The latin name rosmarinus means 'sea dew', perhaps from the appearance of the bush in full flower. The Greeks, Romans and Arabs wove branches of Rosemary into triumphal garlands. The patois name is *du rosmarin*. It was considered to bring good luck, and was planted in most gardens to keep witches away. The plant must never be bought, but must always be grown for one, or given by a well-wisher, and perhaps this gave rise to the saying "Rosemary for Remembrance".

A Herbal written in 1589 by Guernseyman Thomas Andros, grandfather of one of the former Governors of Alderney, noted under Rosemary; 'One makes charcoal from it, with which to draw pictures'.

1 *Rofmarinum Ceronarium*. Garden

1 *Saluia maior*. Great Sage.

Sage

Salvia officinalis is the third shrubby Southern European evergreen plant in this group. Known locally as *d'la saouche*, or *la sauge* in Jersey, it is a plant dedicated to Jove. It was thought to prolong life, increase wisdom, and improve the memory. It prefers a light dry alkaline soil in a sunny position, and flowers June/July.

As far as medicinal properties are concerned, these are shared by the herbaceous biennial **Clary**, or Salvia verbenaca *d'la p'tite saouche* in Guernsey, or *d'l'herbe à la danme* in Jersey. 'Small Sage'.

It is native, and grows wild in Alderney on the sandy commons. The Guernsey plant is often the closely allied Salvia Marquandii. Both plants flower from May to August.

Comfrey

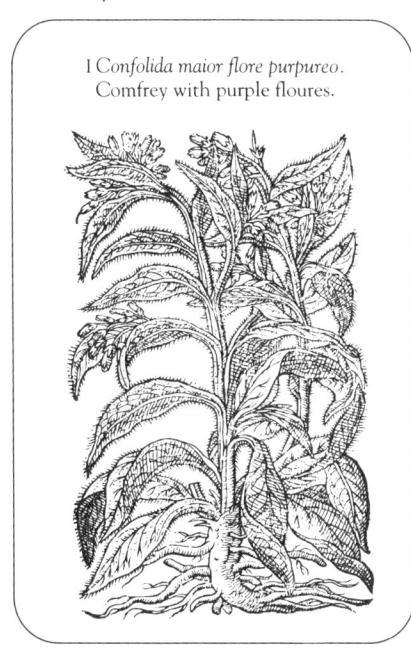

I Confolida maior flore purpureo.
Comfrey with purple floures.

Known in the Guernsey patois as *du Grande Consoule* the great comforter, or in Jersey as *pid d'ouaisé, or le consôle*. The Jersey name comes from the resemblance of the first leaves to a bird's foot. Its roots had to be dug up carefully without breaking even the smallest part, or the effectivness was destroyed. There are two similar species found wild in the islands, both herbaceous perennials. The native *Symphytum officinale*, flowering May-July, and *S. x uplandicum*, or **Russian Comfrey**, first introduced into the islands in the mid 1800s, and now the commoner species. It flowers June-August, and is often grown as a green manure, when composted having similar properties to stable manure.

Rue

Yet another shrubby Southern European. This one is hardy in the cooler northern climate and is also evergreen. It should not be confused with Meadow Rue. Known locally in the patois by the same name *d'la Rue*, and also as *l'herbe d'grâce*, it reputedly had the power of developing second sight or *lé povouaer dé veis dillian*. Also known in England as the 'Herb of Grace', it should be planted in a sunny open place on well-drained rough soil, and flowers in July and August.

I Ruta bortenfis.
Garden Rue.

Wormwood

A Herbaceous perennial with a woody base, this is native, grows on waste ground and in verges, and is usually only found near the sea. It is quite common in Alderney. It is a member of the daisy family and has inconspicuous brownish flowers in July and August.

It probably gets its name from Artemesia, Queen of the Carrians, a noted herbalist in her day. She was the wife of Mausolus, and when he died was consumed with grief. She erected a tomb to his memory, from which we get the word mausoleum, and died of her grief. Because of this, the plant, which provides absinthe, is held to cause melancholy.

1 Abfintbiuum latifolium five Ponticum. Broad leafed Wormwood.

It is known locally as *d'la iaune*, *allaenne*, or *alienne* in Guernsey, and as *d'l'absinthe* in Jersey.

Marjoram

There are three types of Marjoram; the wild plant or **Oregano**, is a perennial growing about a foot high in rough dry, calcareous grassland and on roadside verges. It flowers in August/September, but is rarely found in Alderney.

Marioranamaior Anglica. Pot Marierome.

Pot Marjoram is commonly cultivated. It is a hardy perennial about 2' high and flowers about the same time. Both have similar medicinal properties, and are known in the patois as *d'la marjolaine*.

Sweet Marjoram is an Eastern mediterranean half-hardy annual, mainly used for flavouring, it prefers a neutral soil.

Finally we come to **Vervain**

The last of these nine healing herbs, a herbaceous perennial, occasionally found wild in the islands. It grows to about 2' and has spikes of small pink flowers in July/ August. It local name is *la campana*, or also as *d'l'herbe d'grâce*.

It was considered a holy plant possessing diverse powers. It was also much used in counter spells against withcraft, and was believed to bring good luck.

The Guernsey Herbal already referred to notes; 'If it should happen that some serpent should enter into the body of a labourer, or one of one's people, while sleeping with the mouth open in the fields, gardens or other open places, ... To drink a mixture of Vervain with white wine is a thing to be tried'.

Thomas Sauvary mentions it as one of the remedies used to treat cramp in cows and, according to Gerard's Herbal was known in his time as Juno's Tears, Mercury's Moist Blood or the Holy Herb. It likes a sunny spot on well drained soil.

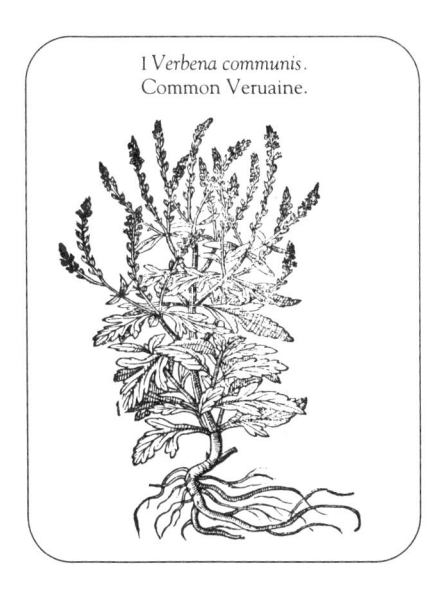

1 *Verbena communis*.
Common Veruaine.

In the remainder of this book, the latin names, as well as the common English and the local patois names will be given for each species, to ensure accurate identification and avoid confusion.

2. Domestic and Medicinal Uses of plants;

The manuscript **Book of Gardening and Medical Secrets**, referred to in the previous chapter and now in the Priaulx Library in Guernsey, was written in the Elizabethan period 'good' French, by Thomas Andros of Les Annevilles in 1589. Translated by Doris C. Cook, it gives a large number of remedies involving plant and animal materials, and some extraodinary horticultural, cosmetic, and culinary suggestions. I am grateful to the library, and to Miss Cook for permission to use extracts from her translation, which are preceeded in the text by an asterisk '*'.

The Jersey material has, in the main, come with their kind consent from the 1896 Bulletin of La Société Jersiaise, where, in an article by E. Duprey, under the title of **Recettes Médicales d'autrefois à Jersey**, many remedies from two old manuscript 'house books' of remedies and recipes, both written part in French and part in English, are set out. One is dated 1633, and was written by Doris Forthe. This volume appeared to be the sixth in a series, copied from books that were old even then, possibly from the Middle Ages. Extracts from this article are preceeded by '+'. Several of these remedies are used in the other islands as well, and others appear again in later publications in Jersey. A number include such diverse materials as earthworms, snails, cow-dung, urine, and eggs.

Undoubtedly many of the more common remedies to be found in most old herbals were also tried in the islands. In general these have not been included here and only the local Channel Island uses of many plants are given in the lists which follow.

The plants involved are presented in the same taxonomic sequence as the latest British Floras. The common English name is given first in bold type, followed by the Latin, both in normal upright type and then the local Norman-French names given in italics, followed by (G) or (J) to indicate which language. The names in Alderney and Sark are generally the same or very similar to the Guernsey names, with minor differences in spelling, which can also occur between the different parishes in both large islands.

1. SEAWEEDS

As in most island communities, seaweeds were used in former times as a source of food. The principal ones were **Sea Lettuce**, Ulva lactuca; **Carrageen**, Chondrus crispus; and **Laver Bread**, Porphyra umbilicalis. This practice had more or less died out, but was revived during the German occupation of the islands during the Second World War. It was gathered in those parts where islanders were able to get to the beaches, many of which were cut off by barbed wire and heavily mined.

For centuries, the heavy brown seaweeds were much used, (and still are to some extent), as a source of fertiliser and fuel, and the customs concerning its collection are detailed in part 5.

I have only come across one reference to a seaweed being used for medicinal purposes.

Bladderwrack, Fucus vesiculosus; *du vraic cossai, du gergeis, cosse dé vraie* (G).

This seaweed was placed in a jar, and soaked in rum for three months. The resulting mixture was used throughout the islands as an embrocation for children with muscular weakness or rickets.

2. FERNS

Black Spleenwort, Asplenium adiantum-nigrum; *du p'tit capillaire*.
Made into a tea will ease a cough.

Bracken, Pteridium aquilinum; *d'la fouaïlle*, where English was used in the islands, generally referred to as 'fern'.

As well as bedding for animals, bracken was used for fuel. It was the principal plant used to cover the *lliet-de-fouâille, jonctière* (G), or *joncquière* (S and A), *liet d'fouailles* or *la filyie* (J); the green-bed or day bed of the Channel Islands, in general use at least to the end of the Great War, and still in common use until the Second World War, beyond which few have survived. These were a wooden platform with boxed sides, about 5'6" x 2'6", and 18 inches high, built beside the chimney, thickly covered in bracken, pea-haulms (*p'sais*), or rushes (*jonc*), and used by the women whilst knitting or telling stories at the veillées or winter social evenings. They were specially dressed on Midsummer Eve, (see below). Those possessed by members of the better classes often had a hessian bag or *paille d'avoine* stuffed with dried seaweed which had been broken up fine, or oat husks etc. on top of the slats first.

Some seventy have survived in Guernsey, a small number in Sark and Jersey, but none in Alderney.

3. FLOWERING PLANTS

Bay, Bay leaves, Laurus nobilis; *fieille d'laurier* (G), *louothi, louothyi* (J).
Used throughout the islands as an appetite stimulant, and a poultice for rheumatic complaints. In the local parler, the name *Laurier* means stye, and an infusion of the leaves was used for bathing styes.

Laurus.
The Bay tree.

White Water-lily, Nymphaea alba;
+ The root of White Water-lily dried and powdered, and as much as would cover a shilling was given with rose jam, plantain water or beer night and morning, as a treatment for scrophula.

Hellebore, Helleborus viridis; *La poumillière*.
For treating consumption in cattle, pierce the dewlap or the ear, and insert a piece of the root in the hole. The resulting abundant suppuration produced sometimes proved beneficial in treating the lung disease.

Buttercups, Ranunculus spp.; *piépot, pi dé Yon, bouton d'or* etc., (G), *du pipot* (J).
Buttercup ointment for piles, or inflammation of any part except the eyes; 1lb. fresh hog's lard, 1pt yellow petals and stamens of buttercup flowers. Melt on a slow fire and boil gently for a quarter of an hour. Strain, and it is fit for use when cold. Rub well into the affected part, preferably in front of the fire.

Goldilocks Buttercup, Ranunculus auricomus;
+ The juice of the 'crowfoot' used to mix a paste of burnt allum, borax and plaster ground together, was used three times a day to annoint sores.

Lesser Spearwort, Ranunculus flammula; *douve* (G), *mailettes* (J).
Water distilled from this is said to have been the preferred local method of causing instant vomitting in cases of poisoning.

Hemp, Cannabis sativa; *Han, Cannivet,* or *Canvre* (G), *cannevi* (J).
Grown for making ropes, canvas, and mats.

Fig, Ficus carica; *figue* (G), *figue, fidgi* (J).
Figs grow well in the generally frost-free climate of the Channel Islands, and stunted trees are sometimes to be seen growing on the cliffs. It was often planted near pigsties, where the heavy foliage gave good shade to the sty, and the roots were well nourished by the seepage from the pig manure. Fine crops of figs resulted.
* 'Engraved figs; Write whatever you want on the eye of the fig-tree which you wish to graft, and the figs which will come from it will have the writing on them'. An old Jersey cure for cancer was to boil five Turkey figs in new milk until tender, split them and apply as a poultice to the affected part, as hot as possible. Each time the poultice was changed, (three times a day), the area was washed with some of the milk, and a quarter pint of the milk had to be drunk night and morning. This was kept up for at least three or four months.

Ficus..
The Fig tree.

Nettles, Urtica spp.; *Ortie, pique-pique* (G), *d's ortchies, d's ortchies grégeaises* (Small or 'fierce' nettle), (J).
The sting of the nettle was referred to in Guernsey as *la pitchaeure d'ortie*, and the rash produced as *le faeu*. Nettles were used at one time as a vegetable, and a tea *thé d'orti* made from the leaves was good for skin complaints, including morphew, leprosy, gangrene, manginess and itch, and was used as a blood purifier.
An old Jersey recipe book, in addition to the above, notes that the tea cured pleurisy, it cures wheezing and shortness of breath, breaks up phlegm, and is used as a gargle for quinsy. It was also good for blood pressure, rheumatism and shingles.
The pressed juice was to be used for healing inflammation of the mouth and throat, cured gravel, stone, worms in children and the bite of a mad dog. Mixed with salt, and rubbed on the forehead it would cure lethargy.
* The Elizabethan MS notes that; 'their juice drunk makes one urinate and breaks up stone. Liniment made from the leaves, salt, and oil, protects all parts of the body from cold and shivering, however great, if one rubs the spine, the soles of the feet, and the wrists with it'.
+ Nettles and eggshells were burnt and the powder blown up the nose to stop a nose-bleed.

Common Stinging Nettle.

Pellitory-of-the-Wall, Parietaria judaica; *d'la pallitôle, parietole* (G), *d'l'apathitouaithe* (J).

Patrietaria.
Pellitorie of the wall.

The peeled leaves of this plant placed over the area as a poultice were commonly used for treating wounds and bruises.

+ 'Take a handful of Pelitory of the wall, boil it in 3pts of conduit watter, about ½ an hour, afterwards strayne it; then put about an ounce of refined sugar & as much of fresh butter, and let be dissolved all together & then put it in a glasse & be sure to doe this composure the 2^d and the 3^d of the moone & dring one halfe seconde and the 3^d day of the moone and let this be done; at the same day you take it & take it warme in the morning fasting, twice that is the 2^d & third of the moone. Probatum est'.

Hazel, Corylus avellana; *cordrillier* (G), *un codriyi* (J).
As elsewhere, hazel rods were used for water divining. the person using them had first to remove every particle of metal from his person. In 1814, the rod was known locally as a *Baguette Divinatoire.*
* 'For surditie [deafness]; take ye water yt falls from ye green hazel boughs ye other end being in ye fire, and mingle it with ye juyce of leeks heads, and drop therof into ye eare, and lye upon ye other eare, doe this often and it will help'.

Beet, Beta vulgaris, B. vulg. ssp maritima; *baette* (G), *des baetes* (J).
* 'The juice of the beets, drawn up through the nose, clears the head. The same juice rubbed on the head kills lice and nits. The root of the beet pounded up and thrown into wine will convert it into vinegar in three hours'.

Love-lies-Bleeding, Amaranthus caudatus;
This garden plant was used in Elizabethan times in Guernsey to deceive drunkards. The flowers steeped in water for an hour turn white and impart their colour to the water making it appear as red wine.

Common Purslane, Portulaca oleracea; *du pourpyi* (J).
Locally known in English as Pot Purslane. * Thomas Andros records that; 'one leaf of this plant put on the tongue will relieve thirst'. The plant was first recorded in Jersey in 1898.

Soapwort, Saponaria officinalis; *des maines jointes* (J).
So called from the jointed rhizome. It was used in the islands to heal wounds in cattle.

Peony, Paeonia mascula;
+ For epilepsy; 'Hang single peony roote about ye neck'.

Tutsan, Hypericum androsaemum; *Toute saine* (Heal All).
As the name implies was used in a large number of remedies.

St. John's-worts, Hypericum spp.; *Trescalan jheloune.*
A balsamic plant, vulneraire and detersive. It was used both to prevent and treat '*phtisie pulmonière*' or consumption.
* 'For wounds in the head; (This is a later entry in English). Take common oyle as much as will fill a strong duble glasse and fill it up full as you can with the buds of St. John's worte, and set in the Sanne [sun] obseuring the same manner as before [this was to set it in the sun for a month, "then kepe it for your vse for any grene wound"] and drop it in as warm as the party can well suffer yet'.

1 *Hypericum.*
S. Johnswort.

Common Mallow, Malva sylvestris; *mauve* (G), *d'la p'tite mauve* (J).
The colour mauve was reputedly named from this plant. As a cure for boils and carbuncles the leaves and stem were boiled, and the juice mixed with bread to make a poultice. The oily juice was supposed to have great healing properties.

Malva fylueftris.
The field Mallow.

Tamarisk, Tamarix gallica; *tameriske, tamérin, saumier, chipre, cipre* (G).
Tamarix wood was used in Guernsey for making the bottoms of lobster pots, because it was very resistant to rotting in sea-water.

Osier, Salix viminalis; *osier, saoud, saud* (G), *d'l'ôsyi* (J).
Not a native plant, but grown in the islands to make lobster pots.

Hedge Mustard, Sisymbrium officinale; *du pid d'ouaisé* (J)
The Jersey name means 'bird's-foot' and refers to the shape of the first leaves. Its wiry stems were said in Jersey to blunt sickles and scythes. A specimen in Gosselin's 1799 herbarium in Guernsey is labelled 'Plante Médécinale', which suggests that this may be the *sensue* or mustard referred to in the MS of Thomas Andros, who says; 'If you soak mustard seed in water and use this to wash the hands, or some other part of the body which needs cleaning, you will see a great improvement'.

Hoary Stock, Matthiola incana; *Violette, Giroufflaie* (G), *d'la violette d'été* (J).
This plant is referred to in Lyte's Herbal of 1578 as 'Gillofers or Garnesee Violets' with obvious direct relations to the patois names. It is found rarely in Jersey as a garden escape, only locally in Guernsey, but is plentiful in Alderney where both mauve and white forms are found, sometimes side by side, but apparently with no hybrids. In Alderney it was believed that if two single stock flowers were tied together exactly at noon on June 24th, (the festival of St. Jean), plants grown from their seed would be double-flowered.

Giant Cabbage, Brassica oleracea longata; *Grande chou à vacque* (G), *chour* or 'Long Jacks' (J).
The Giant Cabbage of the Channel Islands has been grown since at least the 18th century. Its lower leaves, up to 2'6" long, are plucked as the stem extends, and used as cattle feed, 60 plants being sufficient to provide fodder for one cow for three years. It usually flowers in the third year, by which time it may have grown to a height of as much as 12 feet, but more usually about 6 feet. The cabbage head is used to make *soupe à choux*, a staple diet on many farms in the 19th century. The stems, dried and selected, were the basis of a once thriving industry making walking sticks, which is still carried on on a small scale in Jersey. They were also used variously as plant stakes, as a support for thatch over the rafters, and as palisading in the garden.

Cowslip, Primula veris; *coucou*.
+ 'For mad folke; [infusion] of Corduus Benedic [probably **Spear Thistle**, Cirsium vulgare, in the Norman-French *cardaon bêni*]; or Cowslipp flowers given in hot meate & drinke'.

Navelwort, Umbilicus rupestris; *etriqueur, étricoeur* (G), *des cratchillons* (J).
The Guernsey word means 'Heart-render'. It is commonly known in the islands as 'Venus' Navel-wort'.
A peeled leaf was applied to corns in Jersey to remove them.

Houseleek, Sempervivum tectorum; *jaune barbe* (Yellow beard) (G), *d'la jombarbe* (J).
Both mean Jupiter's or Jove's Beard. It is believed to protect houses from lightning if grown on the roof.
* 'If some mouse, spider, fly, wasp, hornet, or other venomous beast, has, by its bite or sting, raised a lump on your flesh, rub the injured part gently with the juice of a houseleek, and immediately the pain and the swelling will be assuaged'.
In Jersey the juice was used as a cure for warts.

Biting Stonecrop, Sedum *acre*; *du grenmil* (G), *du jaune pain à crapauds, pérche-pierre, corinthe à poules, hèrbe ès tuilles* (J).
The first Jersey name meaning 'Yellow Toad's-bread', and *pierre* is used throughout the islands for an upright stone. A tissane of stonecrop mixed with thyme is helpful in treating diabetes.

Large Yellow Stonecrop, Sedum reflexum; *groumil*.
Mixed with garden thyme and made into a tissane was thought in Guernsey to be effective in treating some forms of diabetes.

Saxifrage, Saxifraga spp.;
+ 'For ye stone; take an egg; ye white being put out, fill it with life hony & a little saxifrage water, drink it 2 days before & 2 days after ye full of the moone'.

Dropwort, Filipendula vulgaris;
+ 'For the stone; philipendula, tyme saxifrage, gromwell seede, parsley seed, alexander seed, of each like much; dry them & make pouder of them & use it in drink or eate it & this will ease the stone & cause thee to voyd gravel stones'.

Filipendula.
Drop-wort.

Bramble, Blackberry, Rubus fruticosus agg.; *raonche, ronche, bisaons, maeurier, meuriex* (G), *ronches, mouaithes* (J), *mouriaux* (A).

The rooted stolons of bramble are known locally as *pids d'cats* from the likeness of their cluster of rootlets to a cat's paw. A circle or arch was made of the rooting runners, and a sufferer from boils and other skin eruptions was made to pass through this nine times on nine consecutive mornings whilst still fasting to 'scrape off' the affliction. The runners, then known as *d'la lliache,* were also used to tie bundles of furze together for use in the bread ovens.

Rabus.
The Bramblebush.

+ 'For canker in the mouthe; Take leaves of woodbinde, bramble, sage, rosemary, prime, periwinkle, daisy root and all, herb grace, of each a handfull.

Put them into a quart of wine vinegar, boil it to the consumption of a 4th part, then put to it roche allum the quantity of a walnut beaten small, & a spoonfull of honey; then take it of the fire & set it on a pan of coles that it may boil; let the patient hould his mouth open over it half an hour so nere it as he may well endure & longer if he can; let his head be covered with a sheet that the steame of the liquor go not forth while he is dressing, that that which runneth out of his mouth may run into the medicine.

When he hath done that let that runs out of his mouth be skimd of. Dress it morne and even till he be well. When it is boiled away put in a little more vinegar.

For a childe put in less herbe grace. He may hould up his head to take air when he will, in time of dressing.

Tormentil, Potentilla erecta; *l'herbé de paralysie, quinquacée* (G), *d'l'hèrbe à paralysie* (J).

This is good for treating quinsy, and for treating or preventing paralysis. It was reputedly more effective in men, whilst Milkwort was to be preferred

Agrimonia.
Agrimonie.

for treating women. Some old people took it as a tea to ward off strokes, or to restore speech after one.

Strawberry, Fragaria x ananassa; *Frâse*.
* '... the juice pressed from the fruit is a sovereign remedy for the redness and small cracks which appear on the face from the heat of the fire. The same will relieve redness of the eyes, and clear away the sores and pimples of leprosy'.

Agrimony, Agrimonia eupatoria; No Norman-French name found.
It was used to treat jaundice, colic, and agues (malaria). Mixed with hog fat it will draw out splinters and thorns.

Blackthorn, Prunus spinosa; *nère épaegne* (G);
To treat jaundice, gather branches of Blackthorn, wash, scrape the bark and boil to make a tissane.

Quinces, Cydonia spp. or Chaenomeles spp.;
* 'Pistol wound; To draw out the ball miraculously, make a poultice from quinces, or if lacking these simply use quince marmalade, smear it with olive oil and put it on the wound'.

Apple, Malus spp.; *la paomme*.
The apple is still used to cure warts. It is cut in half and rubbed well on the warts, the two halves are then put together and buried, with no-one being told where. As the apple rots, so the warts disappear.

Hawthorn, Crataegus monogyna; *aube epaenne, bllànche epaenne* (G), *blianche êpingne* (J).
A Jersey cure for jaundice was to go to a house on the right of the gates of St. Ouen's church, where a Thorn bush grew inside the front wall. With the owners permission take a piece of the wood and scape it in a bowl, cover with White Cognac and allow to stand overnight. Strain through muslin and drink a wine glass full twice a day.

Kidney Vetch, Anthyllis vulneraria; Known locally as 'Ladies' Fingers', common in Alderney and Jersey, this is rare in Guernsey. It does not seem to have a patois name recorded. The leaves were used to check bleeding from wounds.

Common Restharrow, Ononis repens; *Réglise, Arrête-boeu, rête-boeuf* (G), *du ricolisse en bouais* (J).
The tough black root has a white centre which the children chew as liquorice, hence one of its names. The other means 'stop-ox' referring to it

stopping the plough from pulling by its spreading tangle of roots just below the surface of grassland.

Tree Lupin, Lupinus arboreus; *lupins* (G), *d'l'abre à lupins* (J).
* 'To remove blemishes from the face mix the pollen of lupins, goat's gall, lime juice, and strong white alum. Touch the marked places with this unguent'.

Under the name of White lupin, peasants used to make a flour from it, treated to make it safe to eat, and then made into a coarse bread.

Broom, Cytisus scoparius; *genêt*, etc.
+ 'A very good recipe for a cold; Take green brrome and dry it over the fire till it be dry and hott, then stand upon it till it be cold and then heat it againe till it hath bine heated. Three times in that manner stan uppon it wth your bare feete, or with your stockings one, and soe soone as it is heated you must stand upon it till it be cold soe it must be done three times before you leave off'.

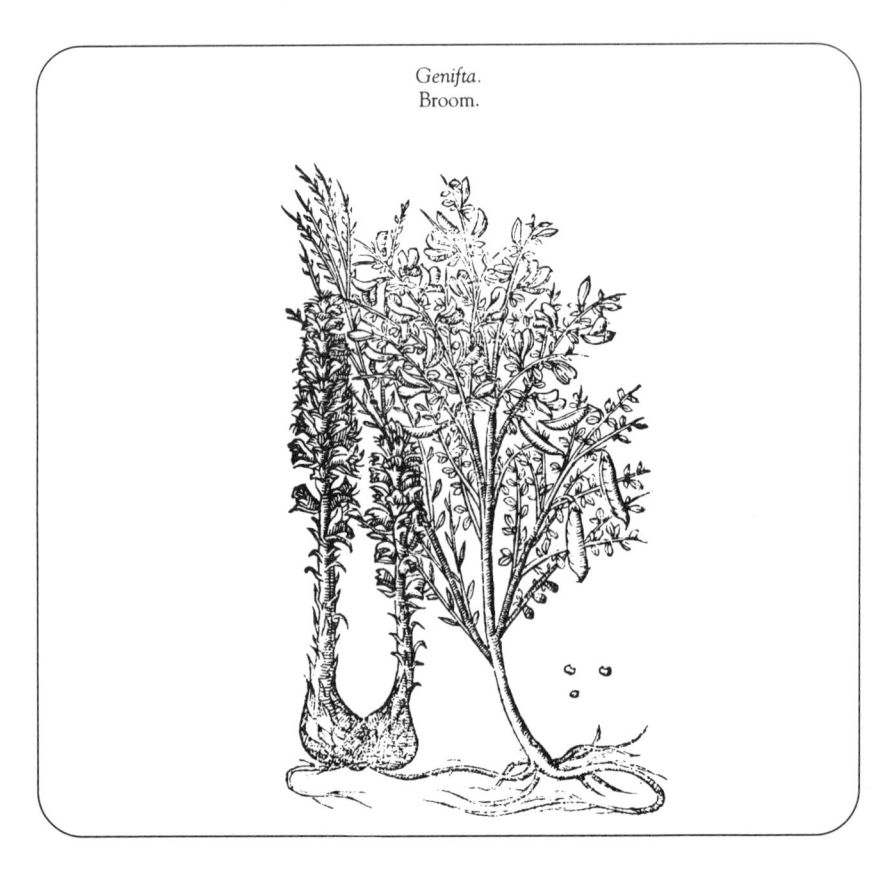

Genifta.
Broom.

Sun Spurge, Euphorbia helioscopia; *la fouirole, herbe à la biche*.
Has strong purgative properties as the local name implies.

Tithymalus Heliofcopius.
Sunne Spurge.

Caper Spurge, Euphorbia lathyris; *d'l'hèrbe d'chorchi* (J).
It was planted in Jersey gardens as a deterrent to witches, and was also thought to keep moles away. There are no moles in Guernsey, and it was not used there.

Milkwort, Polygala vulgaris; *squinancie, coucou dé jaonnière, herbe de paralysie* (G), *d'la stchinnancie* (J).
It was believed to be more effective in treating paralysis in women than Tormentil. The English **Squinancywort**, (Asperula cynachica) is virtually unknown in the islands.

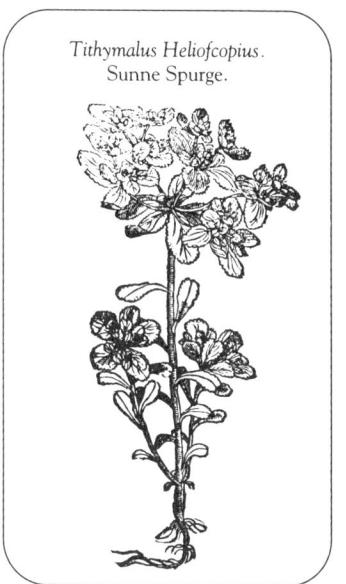

Rue, Ruta graveolens; *l'hèrbe d'grace, d'la rue* (G), *la rue* (J).
One of Guernsey's 'Nine Healing Herbs', it was used as a poultice for sore eyes, and was credited with giving the user *le pouvouaer dé veis dillian* (second-sight).
* 'They say a wonderful thing about this herb: if a woman who is upset in her body, or who has her period, touches this plant, or approaches anywhere near it, she will immediately get better'.
+ 'A precious water that if a man or woman had lost ye sight 10 years, if it be possible they shall recover it againe within XL dayes; Take smallage, rew, fennell, vervyn, agrimony, betony, scabious, avens, hounds tong, eufrage, pimpernell & suage; still all these together with the urin of a male child & 5 greynes of frankincense & drop fore drops of that water every night in the sore eyes & they shal be whole & have sight againe by the blessing of God'.
+ 'For ye canker & for ye gout that festered; ye juice of rue & mint, hony & + of each a like quantity, mingle & boyle ym together on a soft fire of coles still stirring them; if it boyle too fast take it from ye fire till it creame then sett it over again, letting it seeth till it run like pitch then spread it on a cloth & lay it to ye sore as hot as ye sick may suffer it & this will heale it. pbat est'.
+ 'A Metson for the stone in the kidneys; In ye month of ** when the sunne is an oure high, cut earbe of grace otherwise caled Rue, then still it, then restill it, put it into a glase vial and store it close; then tenne

mornings togethere drinke ten spoonefulls and then tenn mornings forbeare and walke after the receaving of it to warm it in your stomake.'

Musk Stork's-bill, Erodium moschatum; *Bec de Grue, epiles ès bergiers* (Shepherds pins), *musque sauvâge* (G), *d's êpîles à chorchièrs* (J).
The names 'Shepherd's' and 'Sorcerer's Pins' comes from the appearance of the fruits, which they were thought to use for this purpose.

Ivy, Hedera helix; *coutinho, yerre, hierre* (G), *du dgèrrue* (J).
Ivy figures in an inhalation remedy in the notebook of Elie Brévint, Minister of Sark from 1612-74. 'For heaviness of the head. Take a handful of mullein and as much of ivy, and boil them in a saucepan without any outlet, in water and vinegar half and half with which ? regli and 3 or 4 figs. Then put over the saucepan a funnel which will cover it; with head covered and mouth open breathe in the steam from this funnel, which will make you sweat a great deal. Reheat the water for three more times'.
The fruits were boiled and eaten during the German Occupation 1940-45.

Garden Chervil, Anthriscus cerefolium; *cherfieil, chue* (G), *le chèrfi* (J).
This plant was credited with blood-cleansing and diuretic properties, promoted sweating, and was used as a poultice for bruises and rheumatic swellings.
+ 'Por guarir dartes humides & coulantes (to heal wet and running skin diseases); [I have translated the remainder] take tanner's water, 3lb chervill leaves, and a pound each of bay and sellisdone [Chelidonium majus] (in English **Greater Celandine**) leaves, boil them down to half; afterwards add 2 ozs. English honey, 6 drachms allum. Foment the affected part frequently with this, as hot as the patient can stand'.

Rock Samphire, Crithmum maritimum; *perchepierre, casse-pierre* (G), *d'la pèrche-pièrre* (J).
As in many coastal areas, the leaves were pickled and eaten.

Fennel, Foeniculum vulgare; *du fanoué* (G), *le fanon* (J).
Widely used in cooking to stimulate the appetite and aid digestion, Fennel was also used as a poultice for inflamed and sore eyes, and was believed to improve the sight.
* 'Its seeds and flowers drunk with milk or wine, will kill worms.'

Parsley, Petroselinum crispum, P. sativum; *du persi*.
Both the wild and the crispy-edged garden varieties, in addition to their culinary use, were used to ensure fertility. Bunches were worn under the arms by men, and large quantities of parsley tea were drunk by married couples. The tea was also believed to improve the complexion. There is a

belief in Guernsey that it is extremely unlucky to transplant parsley as serious injury or death will occur within a year to the offender or a member of his family. In Jersey women with milk fever were treated by bandaging two handsful of parsley under each armpit.

Angelica, Angelica spp.; *du graslard* (J).
Wild Angelica is only found in Jersey, so it is likely that this reference from the 1589 Guernsey Herbal refers to the cultivated variety. 'Whoever will take a little piece in his mouth, or who will drink in the mornings just two fingers of wine and rosewater in which it has been soaked, will never be infected by bad air all the day. Its root, put in a hollow tooth, appeases the pain, and if chewed makes the breath sweet'. It was believed to be one of the strongest protections against witchcraft.

Angelica fylueftris.
Wilde Angelica.

Hogweed, Heracleum sphondylium; *Tchlaise, poîn-feis, tchiesse, caisse* (G), *d'la bênarde* (J).
In Guernsey, in the days of tinder-boxes, the country people used to make matches of the dried stems, split into narrow slivers and dipped in sulphur.

Carrot, Daucus carota or D. carota ssp. maritima; *cârotte, êtue* (G), *d'la cârotte sauvage* (J).
Sliced carrots, covered with brown sugar and allowed to stand in a warm place for several hours, take a spoonful of the juice three times a day. This was used in both Jersey and Guernsey in the treatment of coughs.

Duke of Argyll's Teaplant, Lycium barbarum; *Epäenne d'Aurigny* **(Alderney Thorn)** (G).
A vigorous, salt-resistant, suckering, hedging plant, native of China. Grown close to the sea as a windbreak, it was introduced to Guernsey from Alderney before 1850, and first noted 'in the wild' in Jersey about 1896.

Black Nightshade, Solanum nigrum; *Crêve-coeur* (G), *du vèrjus au dgiâbl'ye* (J),
The Guernsey name means 'Broken-heart' and the Jersey name means 'Devil's grapes'. The plant was used as a narcotic and diuretic for heart complaints.

Potato, Solanum tuberosum; *patates*.
A Jersey remedy for a sore throat was to boil two or three potatoes in their jackets, press them into a gentleman's sock which had just been worn and wrap it round the throat. Leave until quite cold before removing.

Thorn-apple, Datura stramonium; *Pommier du djable, graines du djable* (G), *ponmiyi du dgiâbl'ye* (J). (Devil's apples).
This poisonous plant, very infrequently found 'in the wild' in the islands, was grown, and the leaves and stems dried and smoked like tobacco as a well-used remedy for asthma.

Stramonium pinofum.
Thorny Apples of Peru.

Dodder, Cuscuta epithymum; *herbe d'emeute* (G).
Guernsey farmers used a handful of dodder rolled up in a fresh cabbage leaf to treat some ailments in cattle.

Comfrey, Symphytum officinalis, or **Russian Comfrey**, S. x uplandicum; *du Grande Console* (G), *pid d'ouaisé, le consôle* (J).
The latter was introduced into the islands in 1870, and is now the most common form found. The Jersey name comes from the resemblance of the first leaves to a bird's foot. Its roots had to be dug up carefully without breaking even the smallest part, and were then pounded and used as a poultice, supposedly efficacious in treating lumbago, sores, bruises, and wounds.

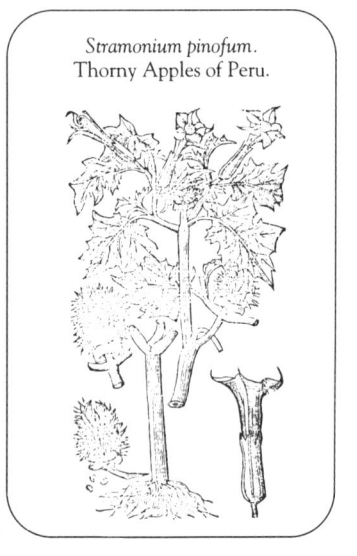

Bugloss, Anchusa arvensis; *Bourrage sauvage* (G), *d'la p'tite g'linne* (J).
* The 1589 MS notes that; 'wine in which leaves of Buglos have been steeped, will take away all sadness'.

Borage, Borago officinalis; *du bouarâge* (G), *le bouôrrhage* (J).
Known as the Herb of Gladness. The juice was drunk to dispel melancholy, and the flowers were used in salads.

Vervain, Verbena officinalis; *la campana, d'l'herbe d'grâce* (G), the latter only is used in (J).
Considered a holy plant by the Druids, and possessing diverse powers. It was in considerable use medicinally, in cleansing wounds, treating dropsy, jaundice and gout, and in the treatment of stomach worms. It was also

much used in counter spells against withcraft, and was believed to bring good luck.

In Jersey it was used to treat the 'King's Evil', *escroilles* or scrophula, and the manner of using it was important. + 'uproot a plant taking care that not a single fibre remains in the ground, then cut off a piece of the root and hang it round the patient's neck with a white ribbon. Burn the remainder of the root. Now hang the foliage of the plant in the chimney, and as it dries the malady will disappear'.

- \+ This remedy was partly written in latin. 'For the treatment of tertian fever; take 1lb each of vervain, and great nettle, pounded and mixed with vinegar, and applied to the wrists before a paroxysm, renewed after 24 hours and again for each subsequent paroxysm.
- \+ 'To draw a boyle from one place to another; Take oculus Christi [probably **Elecampagne**, Inula helenium], and vervyn and make a plaster of y^m, lay y^t from ye boyle 2 fingers brode and do thus 4, 5, or 6 tymes till it come to ye place where you will have it to breake'.

Motherwort, Leonurus cardiaca; *picot*.
A handful of leaves, mixed with half a dozen scales of Houseleek is pounded up. The juice is strained and mixed with a little milk. It was used in Guernsey to treat sick pigs.

White Horehound, Marrubium vulgare; *orâne*.
A tissane of this was greatly prized in Guernsey as a remedy for coughs and colds.

Balm, Melissa officinalis; *du piment*.
An infusion of the leaves was drunk by country folk in Guernsey as a restorative, and the bruised leaves, mixed with salt were used to season the bee-but (or hive), before a new swarm was put in.

Basil, Clinopodium spp.;
Wild Basil is virtually unknown in the islands, but it is widely grown as a garden or pot herb. In Elizabethan times in Guernsey it was reputed that a woman in labour who held a root of basil, together with a Swallow's feather in her hand, would at once be delivered without pain.

Wild Marjoram and **Pot Marjoram**, Origanum vulgare, and O. majorama; *d'la marjolaine*.
Both plants were widely used for stomach upsets, cleansing the blood, headaches, as diuretics, and as a calminative, etc. The oil from the plant, dropped into a hollow tooth, was used in treating toothache. Ointment made from the powdered leaves relieved swollen joints.

Thyme, Thymus spp; *la thaëme* (G), *la thymbre* (J).
Garden thymes were used as a pain killer for toothache, to suppress coughs, and as a cosmetic.

Wild Thyme, Thymus praecox; *cassidone* (G), *d'la serpiliéthe* (J).
Known in Guernsey from Elizabethan times as 'Mother of Thyme' it was used for treating womb infections.

Pennyroyal, Mentha pulegium; *Pouillet, herbe à pouileux, pouiyé, poue-yé* (G).
This plant occurs in a few places in Guernsey, but is unknown or very rare in the other islands. * Andros' Herbal notes that 'the seed if chewed and kept in the mouth will, by its heat, cause the mouth to water copiously. Soaked in vinegar and held in the mouth, it will relieve toothache'. It was also believed in the island that it was efficacious in removing head vermin from children.

Pulegiumregium
Pennie Royall.

Garden Mints, Mentha spp.; *d'la mente, du bouillet* (G), *du menthe* (J).
Garden mints were used as an aid to digestion, and as a compress for rheumatic complaints.

Garden Lavender, Lavandula spp; *d'la casidounne* (G), *la cassidonne* (J).
Another of the 'Nine Healing Herbs' of Guernsey. Used in a wide variety of herbal remedies, and believed to prolong life.

Rosemary, Rosmarinus officinalis; *rosmarin*.
+ 'A very good medison for to horden the nepples before they be brought a bed; Take a top or to of Rosemary, a piece of allum, a spunfull of hunny and boyle it in halfe a pint of rayne water till it be boyled enufe, then wash your nepples with it, a month before you be brought a bed'.

Sage, Salvia officinalis; *d'la saouche* (G), *la sauge* (J).
A plant dedicated to Jove. A decoction of the leaves of Common Garden Sage was used for a wide variety of purposes, and was thought to prolong life, increase wisdom, and improve the memory. It acted as a diuretic, was good for heartburn, coughs, the liver, and made blood. It was also credited with the ability to expel a dead child from the womb, bring on

menstruation, and turn the hair black. A gargle would cure a sore throat. The juice of the plant, alone, or mixed with other ingredients such as spikenard and ginger was efficacious in treating consumption, mastoid, joint pains, cold in the head, epilepsy, lethargy and palsy. It was also used in poultices.

* 'For odour from the teeth it is good to rub them with sage leaves .....'. 'To render fruitful a woman who is sterile, four days after her period let her drink sage juice, with a very little salt, and let her continue and repeat this several times.'

Wild Clary, Salvia verbenaca; *d'la p'tite saouche* (G), *d'l'herbe à la danme* (J).
'Small Sage', or 'Lady's plant', and its closely related taxon in Guernsey, S. Marquandii, which is now considered to be the same species. This plant was dedicated to Venus, and an infusion was also used for treating women's ills and obstructions. The juice was used in the treatment of rheumatic pains, and of venereal diseases before the introduction of mercury ointment. In Jersey a decoction was considered an infallible cure for heartburn.

Ribwort Plantain, Plantago lanceolata; *amourette* (G), *d'l'ancelée* (J).
The leaves of plantain, pounded with white of egg were used in Guernsey in Elizabethan times to heal burns.

Ash, Fraxinus excelsior; *frêne*
+ [Translated] 'For moonstruck eyes; Take a broken piece of ash pith, mix with marrow-fat and grey salt. Set it to cure over charcoal cinders, then take the salt and puff it in the eyes'. Ash walking-sticks were carried by many farmers to ward off evil.

Great or Black Mullein, Verbascum spp.; *d'la molène*.
Both plants were used as poultices in the treatment of bruises and wounds. Mullein also figure in Elie Brévint's remedy given above.

Common Figwort, Scropularia nodosa; *l'herbe dé cràmpe, orvaïle, orvâle* (G).
Used as an effective remedy for cramp. The same terms were used for other Figworts.

Foxglove, Digitalis purpurea; *des cllatchets* (G), *dé l'ouothelle dé brébis* (J).
As in most places digitalis is used for heart conditions. The Guernsey patois name comes from the practise of children bursting the flowers by clapping them on the palm, between their hands.

Germander Speedwell, Veronica chamaedrys; *herbe terraie, herbe terrée, veronique* (G), *du tèrrêtre* (J).
A tea made from this was esteemed in Guernsey as a remedy for indigestion and stomach pains.

Brooklime, Veronica beccabunga; *veronique* (G), *d'la bêle* (J).
A vulnerary, used with Scurvy Grass and Seville oranges in the formulation of **'Spring Juyce'**, a commonly used ancient remedy.
+ 'For sinews yt be stiff of Goeing or for any otherthing; Take Brooklime, horehound & hypericon & with sheepes tallow make a plaster with swines grease, and lay a hott horse turde to ye sore & ye plaster above it.

Eyebrights, Euphrasia agg.; *l'aphraisie* (J).
Drops of an infusion were thought throughout the islands to make the eyes shine, and increase the range of vision.

Elder, Sambucus nigra; *d'le saëue* (G), *du seu* (J).
As well as being a sacred tree, with the power to ward off evil influences and spells, elder had many medicinal properties. A tea made from the leaves eased stomach pains, a decoction of the flowers improved the complexion and removed freckles, and the inner pith was applied to burns to soothe and heal. A 'champagne' was quickly made from the flowers. After two weeks in the bottle, it had a tremendous sparkle and was drunk at harvest time. The berries were turned into an excellent wine which was also reputed to treat a sore throat.

Cornsalads, Valerinella spp.; (The commoner species in all the islands is V. carinata.) Known collectively in Jersey as *d'la bourse*, and sold in the market in spring up to the last war, as a salad. In Guernsey they have two names, *pourselle* and *bruxette*, and were also used as a salad vegetable.

Spear Thistle, Cirsium vulgare; *grànd cardaon, cardaon bêni* (G), *des soudards* (J).
+ '[translated] A drachm of Venice treacle dissolved with three ounces of water of Chardon Benecdit, is excellent to promote sweating, and also to banish fever'.
+ 'Corduus Benedic tea for mad folk'.

Common Knapweed, Centaurea nigra; *Herbe d'flon* (G), *d'la bourdonniéthe* (J).
Flon means a boil or wen, and the plant was used for treating erysipelas. *Le flon* was also a disease of cow's udders after calving. A handful of the herb is boiled for half an hour, and the udder bathed with it to relieve the hardening.

Smooth Sow-thistle, Sonchus oleraceus; *laiteron* Used generally for all Sow-thistles.
+ 'to kill any wen the juyce of a sow thistle'.

Also used as a cure for warts which only worked if they were counted morning and evening, a note made of their number, and a circle drawn round each in ink. They would then gradually disappear.

Dandelions, Taraxacum spp; *laitraön, pîssenlliet* (G), *pêssenliet* (J).
The names derive from the milky juice exuded, and the fear of island children that if they plucked the flowers they would wet the bed. A decoction of dandelion and dock roots was used to purify the blood. The leaves are full of vitamins and minerals and were much used in salads. During the last war the roots were roasted and ground, and used as a coffee substitute in the islands.

Dens Leonis.
Dandelion.

Cudweeds, Gnaphalium spp., [probably **Marsh Cudweed,** G. uliginosum, the commonest species in Jersey];
+ 'Cudwort; good against ye goute'.

Elecampagne, Inula helenium;
+ 'For burning [burns]; take ye leaves of bugle, primrose, and champani [Elecampagne] & ferns y^t groweth upon ye houses & sheepes dung; take & stampt y^m together & fry y^m with fresh butter & strayne it through a cleane cloth'.

Fleabane, Pulicaria dysenterica; *coummaïre* (G), *d'la Coummère* (J).
Was thought to be a sovereign remedy for various complaints.

Feverfew, Tanacetum parthenium; *épergoute* (G), *du maître* (J).
* 'Its leaves, pounded up and applied over the tooth, or put in the ear on the painful side, will completely relieve toothache'.
+ 'A bath; Take a handfull of fetherfoy, a handfull of hemlocke a handfull of ground ivy and boyle it in a quart of Sissing [a decoction made from the root of *Berle* or *skirret* [**Water Parsnip**, either Sium latifolium or Berula erecta, which were often confused], a quart of beer and boyle it all together and bathe her legs'.

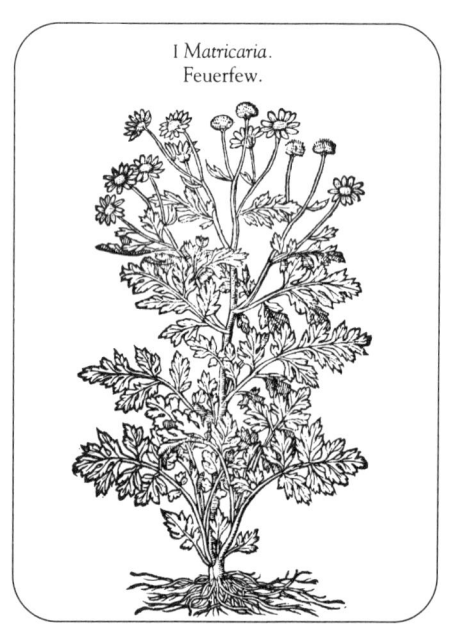

1 Matricaria.
Feuerfew.

Wormwood, Artemesia absinthum; *d'l'allaenne, d'la iaune, iâne* (G), *l'absinthe* (J).
Another of Guernsey's 'Nine Healing Herbs' it was drunk as a tissane to treat stomach troubles, obesity and its attendant ills, and as a marvellous pain-killer. The leaves steeped in water and applied to a new bruise prevent swelling.
It was one of the many ingredients in a very complicated recipe in the old 17th century Jersey books, which was guaranteed to cure leprosy within a year of its onset, and of another, also with a large number of ingredients for dropsy.

Yarrow, Achillea millefolium; *la tchépentchère* (G), *hèrbe au-tchèrpentchi* (J).
The names mean **Carpenter's plant**. Used in the treatment of headaches, coughs, and colds, and for healing wounds.

Oxeye Daisy, Leucanthemum vulgare; *Marguerite, bllanc murlu* (G), *d's ièrs dé boeu* (J).
Marguerite Daisies were thought to have many special healing properties.

Groundsel, Senecio vulgaris; *snichaon*.
For heaviness of the head, take some groundsel, pound it and put the juice in the ear on the worst affected side. Chew in your mouth a piece of toasted bread, which will make yo give off a great deal of the superfluouse humours. (Rev Elie Brévint of Sark, c. 1650).

Winter Heliotrope, Petasites fragrans; *pas d'âne*.
The local name means 'Donkey's hoof' from the shape of the leaves, and should not be confused with the same name in French, which is used for **Tussilago farfara**, Coltsfoot, which is rare in the Channel Islands. The poor people in Guernsey dried the leaves and used them as tobacco.

Marigold, Calendula officinalis; *Soucique, murlu* (G), *la marguérite* (J).
Marigolds were thought to cure cancer and dispel melancholy. The petals were used to garnish soups and salads.
+ 'A good save for a Kibe; Take merigold leaves ingreene, esupe, salarme [**Saltwort**, Salsola kali], prime Rose leaves, camimell. Some beeswax take halfe fresh butter and halfe sheepes suet and beat it all together and boyle it till it bee boyled greene. Boyle the earbes to owres [two hours] and it will be better'.
+ 'For warts; rob yor hands often with ye juyce of marygold leaves & twill make ym fall. Probatum'.

Calendula fimplici flore.
Single Marigold.

Hemp-Agrimony, Eupatorium cannabinum; *d'la jalousie suavage* (J).
Frequent in Jersey and Sark, this plant is only occasional in Guernsey now, and absent from Alderney in the wild. Bushmen from South Africa visiting Guernsey in 1850 recognised it as a plant from which they obtained an intoxicating substance for smoking.

Eel-grass, Zostera marina; *plise, du vézier* (G), *d'la plîse* (J).
Eel-grass was used in Jersey and Guernsey for stuffing mattresses and cushions.

Lords-and-Ladies, Arum maculatum *couaïlle dé prêtre* (Priest's Cow), **and Large Lord's and Ladies,** A. italicum *pilettes*; (G), are both known as *du pitouais* in Jersey.
A. maculatum is absent from Alderney and Herm, and A. italicum, common in Alderney and Jersey is rare in Sark and Herm, and only 'local' in Guernsey. Starch for fine linen was obtained from the tubers of both species.

Soft Rush, Juncus effusus; *joncré, jonc* (G), *du jonc* (J).
One of the plants used to cover the Green-beds or jonctières.

Compact Rush, Juncus conglomeratus; *jonc*.
Although this does not have a separate patois name in the islands and was possibly confused in earlier times with the previous species, it was supposedly the species whose pith was used as a wick in the cottager's *cresset* or oil-lamp in the islands. The oil used was usually obtained from fish.

Galingale, Cyperus longus; *Han*
A number of uses and customs exist for this common plant of damp places. It was used for bedding, both on the Green-bed, and for cattle; for plaiting into mats for the kitchen floor; mixed with clay to form a hard floor; for chair seats; and plaited into cow tethers, halters, horse-collars, and saddles, or used for stuffing other saddles. A Guernsey saddle made of *han* is in the Economic Uses Museum at Kew. *Les Hannièthes* and *La Hanniéthe* in Jersey are named from places where it used to be grown.
An interesting custom known as *faithe braithe les peîles* or *faire braire des poêles* was performed in Jersey on St. John's Eve to keep evil spirits away. A large brass *bachîn* (the traditional boiler in the islands) is filled with water. Metal utensils, preferably of silver, are put in, and the rim of the boiler is tied round with a thick cord of *han*. To this are attached strings of *han*, equal in number to the people present. When these are thoroughly soaked they are pulled tight and the hand run rapidly up and down them. The tremulous vibration caused is transmitted to the contents of the basin or

peîle which causes the metal objects to agitate producing a loud, barbarous, melancholy, sound. This was kept up for hours to drive the spirits away, and was often added to by blowing on cow's horns.

Oats, Trisetum sativum; *avogne, avaigne.*
* 'Blotches on the face; To remove redness of the face, it is good to wash it with a decoction made from the straw of oats and barley, then to bathe it with lemon juice'.

Marram, Ammophila arenaria; *millegreux, milgré* (G), *du melgreu* (J).
As in Normandy this was used in the islands for making brooms, straw hats, and mats.

Common Couch, Elytrigia repens; *du bas, du tchian-dent* (hold-tooth) (G), *du bas* (J).
A tissane of Couch grass was used as a diuretic, and also reputed to be a good remedy for catarrh.

Purple Moor-grass, Molinia caerulea; *du sectin* (J).
In Jersey this was another of the plants used for bedding on the jonctières. In Guernsey tobacconists used to sell the stems for cleaning pipes.

Common Reed, Phragmites australis; *rôs.*
Used for thatching, it was much more durable than straw and lasted up to 80 years.

Onion, Allium cepa; *ougniaon, ouogniaon.*
* 'For bumps and bruises. Strip an onion of its outer leaves with your hands, no metal must touch the onion, and place it in a bowl and crush with a piece of wood until pulped. Put the pulp in a piece of muslin and place it on the bruise which will disappear'.
+ 'For wormes in a man's eares y[t] hinder him from hearing; An onion cored & filled w[th] hony set it at ye fire & being warme strayne it through a cloth & mingle w[th] it juyce of plantayn & drop into ye eares & let him lye so 1 day or half a day w[th]out meate or drink & it shall stray all ye wormes that hinder hearing, also w[th]out hony it strays sheeps lice crept into ye eares'.

Three-cornered Garlic, Allium triquetum; *bllanche côneille, l'ail* (White Bluebell), (G), *d'l'as sauvage* (Wild Garlic), (J).
Known throughout the islands as 'Stinking Onions', this Mediterranean plant seems to have been introduced in the early 1800s. It is now abundant everywhere, and the bulbs are sometimes used as a substitute for garlic.

Garlic, Allium sativum; *d'l'ail*.
+ 'For surditie [deafness]; A peece of a clove of Garlick dipped in honey & tyed wth a thread & put into ye eares at night, and draw it away ye next morning'.
+ 'For a cow in whose tayle wormes are; This is known by the loosening of her teeth. Then take garlic, salt & cobweb, stamp them all together, then slitt the tayle in 4 or 5 places and bind the said things to ye jointes where the worm is (& thou shalt know where the worm is by ye joint, for that joint ye worm is in will be open) so let it lay till it be whole, for twill heale it of warrantise'.

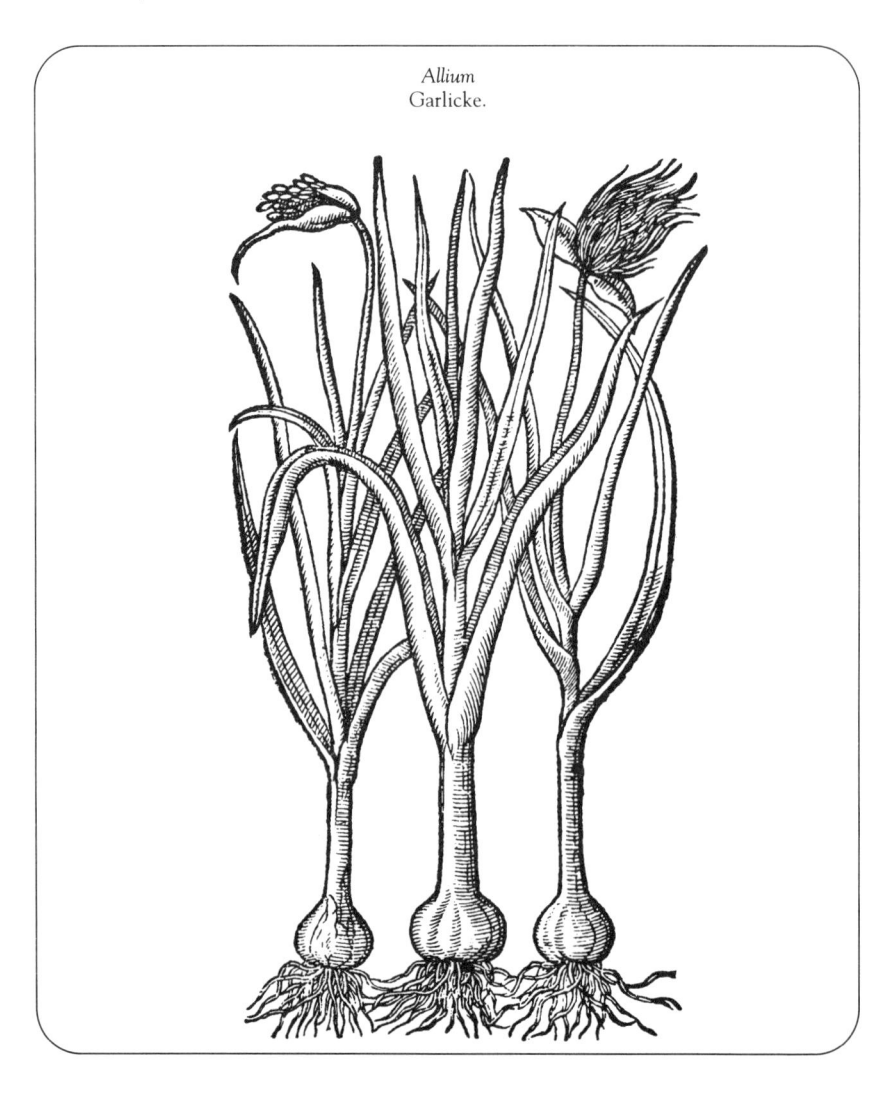

Allium
Garlicke.

Leek, Allium porrum; *pouorraie*.
+ 'For a burn; verjus of grapes & juyce of unsett leeks put together & wett a linen cloth on y^m & lay it upon ye burn half an hower, then anoint it wth oyle of yolke of eggs'.
+ 'For a broken head; Take the juyce of unsett leeks & putt in the wound all night & in ye morning mingle ye juyce wth hony & doe it in the wound & if there be broken bones in it it will draw y^m out & alsao heale the wound'.

Lilies;

Neither **Lily-of-the-Valley**, Convalaria majalis, *Mudget*, nor Narcissus species, *Pourriaön*, are native to the islands, the first mention of Daffodils, brought as a crop from Guernsey, being by Thomas Knowleton in 1726. Daffodils are often referred to as **Lent lilies** in the islands, and are possibly the source of the next remedy, perhaps from gardens, or imported. * Water distilled from the 'lily' flowers was recorded in Elizabethan times in Guernsey as; 'removing wrinkles from the women's faces and making them pure white'.
The two famous local lilies are;
1. the **Guernsey Lily**, Nerine sarniensis, *la Guernesiaise*, referred to by this name by Linnaeus in 1753, whose arrival in the island is the subject of an interesting legend. John Evelyn wrote about its cultivation in 1687 under the heading of '**Japon or Garnzy Lillies**'.
2. the **Jersey Lily**, Amaryllis belladonna, known in the patois as *belladounnes*, or *des belles-tutes-nues* from the flowers arising before the leaves.

Madonna Lily, Lillium candidum; steeped in rum or brandy was a Jersey cure for cuts.

Yellow Iris, Iris pseudacorus; *gllâcheur, gllâcheul* (G), *du bliajeu, Jeujeu* (J).
* 'To remove bad smells from the mouth it is good to chew the root of the yellow iris, or a lump of putty for a sufficient length of time'.

A 19th century Guernsey Recipe for *Pot Pourri* was as follows;
To a bowlful of dried rose petals add a handful each of dried marjoram, thyme, and rosemary. Add two handsful of dried lavender flowers and the grated rinds of a lemon and an orange. To this add five bay leaves and a teaspoon of allspice.

3. Beliefs about the properties of plants;

Lesser Celandine, Ranunculus ficaria; *Piss-en-liette* (G), *morrhouiton* (J)
It was believed in Guernsey that children who picked these flowers then wet the bed.

Common Poppy, Papaver rhoeas; *Rose de T'chen* (Dog Rose) (G).
If placed too near the eyes or ears, could cause blindness or earache.

Fumitory, Fumaria spp., the common Channel Island species being F. muralis subsp. borraei; *feumeterre* (earth-smoke) (G), *finnetèrre* (J).
This plant was supposed to be produced without seed, from smoke arising from the earth.

Oaks, Quercus spp.; *Tchêne*, (*Vert Tchêne* Holm Oak)
The oak was supposed to deflect lightning, and blind cords usually had an acorn carved from oak hanging from them at the windows to keep the lightning out of the house.

Redshank, Polygonum maculosa; *herbe traïtresse, langue d'ouaie* (G), *du paîve à j'va* (horse) (J).
A Guernsey legend has it that the dark mark on the leaves of this plant were caused when a woman who had murdered her husband wiped her blood-stained hands on the leaves of a plant of persicaria. This led to her detection, and ever since the plant has carried the mark.

Perforate St. John's-wort, Hypericum perforatum; *Herbe à mille pertus, trescalan jheloune* (G), *du cache-dgiâbl'ye* (J)
It was hung round the windows on St. John's Eve, so that the 'Thousand Holes' might 'Catch the Devil', as the two names imply. It was also thought to catch lightning.

Roses, Rosa spp.; *raose.*
* 'You will have green roses if you graft the rose tree on to the trunk of an old cabbage [probably the Long Jack or Jersey Cabbage], or on to an oak tree; the roses will have no scent'. 'You will have yellow roses if, after planting the rose tree in the ordinary ground near to a broom-tree, you pierce a hole in the broom with an auger. Then in this hole plant various roots or shoots scraped from across all parts of the rose-tree, which you must bind and fasten to the broom with mortar. When you see that the hole has healed, cut the trunk of the broom above the place where you made the hole and let the rose shoots bloom. By this means you will have yellowish roses'.

Hawthorn, Crataegus monogyna; *Aube Epaôine* (G), *blianche êpîngne* (J). (Often known locally as Whitethorn to distinguish it from **Blackthorn** (Prunus spinosa, *nère-épaegne*). It was also known as *Le roué des bouais*, the 'King of the Woods', in Guernsey.

This plant figures frequently in local beliefs and customs.

It's wood must not be employed for 'common' purposes or uses, and any ship in which it had been used would infallibly be lost, or come to grief at sea.

A *désorceleur* or white witch would make bewitched persons go through certain actions in front of a particular ancient thorn tree at the ruins of Les Annevilles Manor in Guernsey, to remove the curse.

May blossom *d'mai* must never be brought into the house as it brings bad luck with it. The country parishes in Guernsey believed it brought sickness and death with it into the house.

It was used as a *bornement* or boundary marker in former times. They were planted for this purpose by the parish authorities, and there were penalties for anyone removing them.

To destroy or remove the tree would result in divine retribution.

Witches took the forms of hares or rabbits and gambolled below them in the moonlight. In England witches were believed to turn themselves into Hawthorn trees on Walpurgis night.

Apples, Malus spp.; *poummier.*
* 'To get red apples it is necessary to water the tree with urine, or else to plant some roses near the apples'. 'To get red apples plant mulberries very near the apple-tree. Or else drive some stakes into the earth near the tree, and put on them a vessel full of water in such a way that the rays of the midday sun fall directly on it, so that the vapour which the water gives off may circulate around the fruit. Or else, in the spring-time uncover [the roots] of the tree and water it several times with urine; at the end of ten or twelve days earth it up again and water it at intervals with urine'.

Cider making was an important industry in the islands in the 16th-19th centuries, and most farms had a stone cider press worked by a horse. It was customary to bless the trees with cider, and in Jersey **Black Butter** was made, see below.

Broom, Cytisus scoparius; *bringe, g'nêt* (G), *du genét* (J).

To preserve onself against the power of witches, it was necessary to take nine pieces of green broom and tie them together in the form of a cross; place them in a small sack of new linen cloth, with nine leaves each of betony and agrimony. Add a little bay salt, sal ammoniac, new wax, barley, yeast and camphor, and some quicksilver enclosed in cobbler's wax. Sew the sack up so that nothing may fall out and hang it round your neck.

Hemlock Water Dropwort, Oenanthe crocata; *Pain-faie, pôui-faie* (G), *d'la chue* (J).

One of the most poisonous plants, it was eradicated in Alderney about 1850. The Guernsey name means 'fairy bread'.

Fool's Parsley, Aethusa cynapium; *Tue-lapin* (G), *d'la p'tite chue* (J).

Another poisonous plant. In Guernsey it was believed to kill rabbits which ate it.

Rosemary, Rosmarinus officinalis; *du Rosmarin*.

It was considered unlucky not to have one near the house, but the plant must never have been bought. It had to be given, or grown for one by a well-wisher.

Elder, Sambucus nigra; *d'la saeue* (G), *du seu* (J).

The Elder was held sacred, as it was reputedly the wood from which the cross was made. It was planted close to the door of the house to protect the house against lightning, and to exclude witches, and by the dairy door to prevent them interfering with butter-making. People believed that if they stood under an elder tree during a thunderstorm they were protected from lightning strike. Except in Suffolk where it is also considered a holy tree, this belief in the islands is quite contrary to most areas of England, where it is believed that no witch would be without one in her garden and often lived inside it. It must therefore never be grown near a dwelling house, burnt in a domestic fire, or the wood used to make a cradle. If there is any necessity to prune or cut one down apology must first be made to the witch living inside it or dire consequences would result.

CHANNEL ISLAND PLANT LORE

4. Customs involving plants;

The Great Ploughing

Sometime in February, depending on the season, *La Grande Querrue* took place. It was the time for preparing the ground for *pônais* or parsnip-sowing, an important crop in the islands in the 16th-19th centuries. The process needed a very large plough to make the furrow deeper than usual. This custom was carried on a large scale in Jersey and Guernsey, where several of the ploughs have survived, but less in Alderney, as most of the arable land there was given up to the growing of corn, and sadly the plough used there has not survived.

Parsnip-growing, on which tithes had been recorded since before 1500 in Guernsey, had become of major importance there around 1800, and special large ploughs *Les Grande Querrues* drawn by long teams of horses, sometimes mixed with oxen, as many as 22 animals combined, were developed for the deep cultivation this crop requires, the first of these being on Lenfesty's farm in the parish of Le Câtel. This gave rise to a great social occasion at which neighbours combined their teams and worked together using a communally shared plough, and the wives and daughters provided food and cider, to all who came, out in the fields.

April 1st.

On *la jour de foues*, April Fool's Day, <u>after</u> twelve o'clock, the children stuck lengths of **Cleavers**, Galium aparine; *Gratteron, La coue, Herbe d'Satan* (G), *d'l'hèrbe à tchilieuvre* (J), on people's backs. The afternoon was then known as *le jour des coues* (day of the tails).

Le Branchage

Householders, and landowners in the islands are required to keep their hedges bordering public roads cut back to a height of 12 feet, and to 8 feet along public footpaths. This has to be carried out twice a year in a specified 15 day period in July and September. The Parish constables carry out an inspection of all their roads and paths after each period, carrying poles of the required heights. A warning is issued to any offender and, if the fault is not rectified within a week, they can be fined and the work carried out by the parish at their expense. This law is still regularly enforced in Jersey, Guernsey, and Sark, but has largely lapsed in Alderney since the war, when the position of parish constable was discontinued, although the provisions of the law are still published in the Alderney Journal most years. Strangely the height limit there is 15 feet.

Les Brandons

In ancient times the remnants of a pagan fertility rite were celebrated on what later became the first Sunday in Lent, when the young people of the islands, as in many other communities elsewhere, assembled to feast and dance at the time of the spring plantings, in order to ensure the fertility of the crops. They also reputedly made love in their family's fields to ensure their fertility.

In Alderney, this Bacchanalia was held on the tidal islet of Clonque, then only connected by a natural causeway, where they all repaired in their best clothes, with musical instruments, to picnic and dance, play kissing games and make other entertainments. In the evening a huge bonfire was lit, after which they all danced back to the town bearing torches up to 10 feet long, made of rush (or *gluie*), or from twisted straw. They ran through the streets waving these to the great danger of the thatched roofs of the houses. This custom was known as **Les Brandons**, and in the early 1700s the Governor of Alderney tried to have it banned because of the danger to the houses. By about 1800 this pagan custom had become a time for dancing, feasting, singing and exchanging kisses. At nightfall the Brandons, (torches), were lit and the youngsters went in procession to the town. Despite this attempted ban, it continued well into Victorian times, in the late 19th century. It died out early in the 20th century.

A similar custom seems, in later but undated times, to have taken place in September when the harvest was in. This has variously been called *Les Brandons* or *Le Jour des Vitres* (masks).

A possible remnant of this custom appeared in July 1922, when the annual cattle show which had been held in May, June or July since Victorian times, was combined with a week of games and competitions between the Alderney Militia and the Army garrison, and was called 'Alderney Week'. The week finished with a torchlight procession, bonfire and firework display reminiscent of Les Brandons. This custom took hold and continued most years until the Second World War. It was restarted in 1948 and although the cattle shows ceased in the early 1960s, has been held most years since. It takes place in the first week in August, when, unlike the rest of the islands and Britain, Alderney still maintains, the traditional August Bank Holiday on the first Monday in the month.

May

The other May-day festivities died out many years ago, but for occasional revivals of crowning a May Queen and a may-pole at the schools. Formerly the three first days of the month were a time of general recreation, and in the 1840's May Day was an official holiday. About a week before, children went from door to door begging ribbons for their garlands; and during the three days wreaths and hawthorns were hung across the streets after the manner of bunting. There was no May-pole in Alderney, but apparently word went round that "The May will be at So-and-so's today", where a specially large and gaily-ribboned garland would be hung. The regular places where the garlands were hung, were, The Bourgage, St. Martin's, the Marais and Blaggud's Corner.

Thither everyone repaired, the children and young folk during the day, the older people after work in farm and quarry was over. The principal dance was "Le Beau Laurier", danced hand-in-hand in a circle whilst singing traditional songs, which gave place in time to the English kissing game "Sally, Sally, Water".

The celebrations are a remnant of the Feast of the Roman goddess Maïa.

For many centuries in Alderney the first Sunday in May was the traditional time for turning out the cattle into the fields, where, in accord with the custom in the islands they were (and frequently still are) all tethered. The young people would steal a few eggs, and milk the cows where they stood in the fields. Adding rum, cinnammon, and sugar, to the mixture, produced a potent drink known as 'Milk-a-Punch'. This custom continued until the island was evacuated in 1940, and after the war was restarted in a slightly different form by the publicans, who ever since have offered their customers the first drink of their own special recipe for this mixture free on 'Milk-a-Punch Sunday'. The custom was also formerly observed in Jersey, (but apparently not in Calvinist Guernsey), with a similar custom across The Race, on the Cotentin peninsula in Normandy. Known there as the *Lait de Mai* it was kept up until the Great War. The cattle were turned out on 1st May, the milk and eggs were taken, mixed, and drunk, in the field, but there seems to have been no alcoholic element there.

Vraic gathering

The civic customs associated with the start of the vraicing or gathering of sea-weed for fertiliser and fuel are very ancient, and are followed throughout the islands. Vraic was of two kinds, *vraic venant* or drift weed, which could be collected at any season, between sunrise and sunset, and *vraic scié* or cut weed, for which a special hooked sickle was used.

The rules for the collection of vraic scié were controlled by the Court of Pleas, and everyone had to abide by them. It was collected at two seasons. The first was the spring tides after Candlemass (2nd February), which usually meant towards the beginning of March, and went on for several weeks, including the lowest equinoctual tides, when farmers stripped the shores clean of their seaweed, for the annual manuring of the land. Vraic was also known as *varech de fumure*, (fumier, 'manure').

All had to abide by the law of "vraicage", that forbade any gathering of seaweed before the vote of starting had been taken. In Alderney, the bell inside the church tower on the Huret summoned the "vraicers", the Procureur had to be present, and if the weather was stormy there was generally a heated altercation. "J'irons", said those grouped on the right. "J'irons pas!" cried their opponents on the left. Each farmer was allotted his patch of shore, special knives were used to cut the vraic at low water, and his heaps of vraic were marked by initialled stones. His spoil was brought ashore in panniers and conveyed inland in two-wheeled carts. The women brought down provisions to the beach, and prepared another festive meal at home. Nearly a century has passed since the last true vraicing time in 1899. The vraic was left to partly dry out at the top of the shore, and in several of the property transactions between the Crown and the Islanders at various times, a 100 foot wide strip of Government land at the top of the tide was reserved for the use of the inhabitants for this purpose (extended to 100 yards in two places). Several of the carved boundary stones which delineate this area are still to be seen. The vraic was then either spread and ploughed in directly, wherever it was wanted, or burnt in heaps and the ashes used as fertiliser. Today the custom still continues to a limited extent in Jersey and Guernsey, but in Alderney only a very little use is made of seaweed, principally by a few gardeners, and whatever vraic they want is carted at any time after a gale, from the loose material thrown up on the beach.

The second season was at Midsummer, which lasted to about the middle of August. The poor people who had no horse and cart were allowed first cut, and had to carry the weed above the high-water mark on their backs. The piles would then be marked with a flat stone, and no-one else could move them. This material was usually dried, stacked, and used for winter fuel, the ashes of their fires were carefully preserved for their rich mineral content and either used on the person's own land, or sold as a valuable fertiliser. The vraic harvest was then opened to all. Small heaps of weed were cut and marked as the tide fell, and when low-water was reached these heaps were carried away in carts driven across the beaches, or in horse panniers, and dumped above high-water mark to dry. The occasions were made a great time for all the family to help, and feast on the shore, and crabs, ormers and the occasional cuttle-fish, octopus or conger eel, were caught to add to the festivities. When the tide was high and no more could be gathered, dancing was the order of the day for the young people on the grassy shore, and at the waters edge. The vraic was then spread out on the grassy areas to dry.

From early times special vraic roads had been formed in the islands to enable the carts to get down to the beaches. These were well constructed with a cobbled surface, with the setts at an angle to enable the horses' hooves to grip when pulling the full carts up them. Some were destroyed in 1802 as a precaution against possible French landings, some were rebuilt, and there are many, still kept in good condition in the larger islands. Most of the Alderney ones are today in a ruinous condition, with only a few still usable, as at Braye and Clonque Bays, or still showing, part buried in the sand, as at Longis near the Nunnery, and at Clonque.

The use of vraic conveyed a great benefit to the soil. The mass of organic material provided humus which helped considerably to retain moisture in the sandy soils of the islands, and the minerals present giving fertility, which enabled continuous crop-growing on the same ground. Today's use of artificial manures contributes little to the long term structural quality of the soil, and is a source of pollution of the water supplies. It was also much used as a fuel, and the ashes carefully saved to use as fertiliser.

Harvest Customs

When the fields were enclosed in England from the fifteenth century on, similar enclosures were made in Jersey and Guernsey. Alderney however has retained the open field system almost to today.

There, for the harvest period only, the Great Blaye (from *blé*, corn), was divided naturally into three quarters, whilst the Little Blaye made up the fourth quarter. There were also two enclosures on the Huriaux, near Essex Castle; Le Gan, and Le Val. At harvest time there was, by Elizabethan times, and probably earlier, a well established order of proceedure. The need for this was dictated by the multiple ownership of the land within each section of the enclosure. All of the enclosures outside the Blayes were free land, and several of these enclosures were in the hands of a single person.

The laws required all crops to be stacked on the land on which they were grown until the tithes had been gathered, once the corn was cut, bound in sheaves and 'shocked' or 'stooked' to dry, on each of the Riages [strips].

There was a distinction between *terre franche* (freehold land), and *terre vilain* (where the user owed service to the Seigneur), and the areas so designated were clearly delineated by round topped marker stones bearing the letters 'F' or 'V'. These are made of limestone which does not occur in the islands, and were obviously imported specially, presumably from England. A few still remain. The tithes owed to the Fee-farmer, Seigneur, Lord or Governor, (however he was designated at various times), differed. *Champart*, or Champard, payable on Vilain or *champardière* land, consisted of *the "seventh sheaf from each stack, and the fifth from the foot"*, whilst the tithe on free land was, the "tenth sheaf from the stack and the seventh from the foot". There is an interesting account of how some of the Terres Franche and Vilain came to be mixed up in the same enclosures.

It seems that when two lawyers of Queen Elizabeth came to the island as Royal Commissioners in 1585, all of these free lands now within the vilain were then also *champardière* and belonged to a single woman. This lady regaled the Commissioners so freely with currant cake, that, when they left, they asked her what they could give her in return. She asked that her lands should be freed, and it was so ordered.

An Alderney record dated 7th December 1661 notes that 271 vergées of the Blaye were declared as *champardières* or owing tithes. (Approximately $2^1/_2$ vergées equals one acre, the exact area varying between the islands).

For each 'Quarter' of the Blayes, the Seigneur appointed a 'Master' and six, eight, or ten, boys, to record the crops taken, the master was provide with a 'portable' book in which the proper designation of each riage section was recorded to ensure that the correct number of sheaves were collected as each stack or heap was removed, depending on the type of land. The Seigneur's tithe had to be removed and stacked on the riage before any carting could take place to the owners premises. The boys had to walk behind each cart in turn to ensure that the drivers did this.

When all of the corn had been cut and the sheaves bound, the Seigneur had to be advised of this, and set a day for the carrying to begin.

In Governor John Le Mesurier's time, this was carried out in accordance with an act of Chief Pleas (the Alderney twice-yearly Court), dated 3rd November 1791, which simply confirmed the custom already long in existence.

After the sheaves were stacked, the Governor was informed, the tithes counted and separated as the carts were loaded, and the fields then carried away in a prescribed sequence.

1. On the first day the sheaves from La Hoire, Le Gân, and Le Val, only were carted.

2. The sheaves from the quarter of the Cobles to the corner of L'Essource and Vaindif Mollin were carted on the second day.

3. The third and fourth days were given to the Governor's own land, and only those working for him could cart away.

Those inhabitants who possess a team and cart were required to carry for the Governor, and were paid three sous tournois a load.

4. After the Governor's crops were removed, the *riagers* could cart their own crops from sunrise to sunset.

5. The tithes left behind were then carted, and as soon as all of the tithes were at the *hautguard* or stack-yard, the Governor had to cause the bell to be rung to signal that the Blayes were open. Cattle and sheep (but not pigs), could then be put freely on the Blaye until 1st January.

The Mauvaises Herbes Laws

In an attempt to prevent fouling of neighbouring land by bad husbandry, the various *Mauvaises Herbes Laws* were passed in the islands from the 1920s. It became an offence to allow this specified list of plants to be on one's land in flower or in seed, and gave the States power to order their removal, or carry out the work and charge the landowner if he failed to do so after a warning, and to prosecute offenders.
　　The Guernsey Law was passed in 1927, and replaced with another in 1952, leaving out Small Nettle and Wild Garlic;
　　The plants concerned in the 1927 law were;
Hemlock Water Dropwort; Cow Parsnip or Hogweed; Ragwort; Spear, Creeping and Marsh Thistles; Docks of all kinds; both kinds of Nettles, Wild Garlic (Allium Triquetum or Stinking Onions).
　　The similar Alderney law followed in 1933. This, interestingly, also included Hemlock Water Dropwort, common enough in Jersey and Guernsey, but eliminated in Alderney by the 1860s.
　　To this list for Alderney, were added in 1956;
Charlock; Dandelion; and Hedge Mustard.

Carts

At one time all owners of carts in Jersey were compelled to grow flax, presumably to obtain Linseed oil to lubricate their wheels.

Sowing seeds, etc.

There is an old custom in Guernsey, that when a field was finished sowing, a piece of *gâche* (a sort of cake) had to be left in the furrow as an offering to ensure germination.
　　The timing of sowing was also important, and regulated by the moon. Saint's days were favoured for planting, but peas, beans, and grain crops should only be sown on a waning moon, whilst small seeds should be planted on a waxing moon. Vegetable seeds should be planted at the new moon. These customs are still followed by many farmers and gardners in the islands.

Black Butter, *Le nièr beurre*

A Jersey custom since at least Elizabethan times which took place in the late autumn was the making of black butter from apples. This custom, once widespread and a great social occasion on farms, still survives today in one or two farmsteads.
　　Huge quantities of apples were peeled, cored and sliced by the women

during the day, and placed in a huge brass *bâchin* called *la peîle*. By afternoon this was filled, and was placed on a trivet over a fire, and a gallon of cider added for every 70 lbs of apples. Lemon, spices, liquorice, and sugar were added. It then had to be stirred continuously by two or three people, using long wooden rakes, and was kept boiling for the rest of the day and throughout the night.

Neighbours gathered to assist, and the men kept the stirring going, whilst the women produced refreshments, games were played by the assembled company, and the stirring continued. By morning the mixture which was by then thick and almost black, was ladled into jars and bowls and sealed. The helpers were each given a jar, and the remainder was used by the family or sold in the market in white bowls.

Cider

At least two customs are associated with the cider making.
In the spring a certain tree was selected in each orchard, and a group assembled. A libation of the previous year's cider was poured round the base to bless the tree, and to ensure a good crop of apples.

In the autumn, the granite cider presses known as *les touors*, possessed by each farm were brought into use, and family and neighbours again assembled to help with the process of cider making. At the end of October or the beginning of November, when the first batch of cider was ready, everyone drank a toast *à l'honneur du meis d'Octobre*.

Cider making was an important industry in Guernsey and Jersey from the 16th to the end of the 19th century. Writing in 1695, Robert Mordern said;

'Both islands are adorned with many Gardens and Orchards, which supply them with an artificial sort of wine, made of Apples. Some call it Sisera, we Sydre'.

A Guernsey Directory dated 1874 notes that; 'hundreds of hogsheads are annually shipped to England'.

Alderney never had an appreciable number of apple trees at any recorded time in its history, possibly due to its more exposed, windswept position, and their cider was imported from Guernsey.

5. Magic Uses and Love Charms;

The two most important dates associated with charms and spells were the Vigil of St. John the Baptist, otherwise called St. John's Eve, or Midsummer Eve, and St. Thomas's Eve, December 24th. Many of the more common customs were associated either with finding the name or the appearance of a girl's future husband, or with warding off evil.

On St. John's Eve fresh fern was cut for the traditional green bed, which had a canopy raised over it decorated with brilliant, showy, summer flowers, often arranged in elegant patterns, and a young girl dressed in white would sit silent under the canopy to receive the homage of the other women.

In Sark the young swains would bedeck themselves and their horses with bunches of flowers, and set out in search of their loved ones. The girl would be wearing a flower-decked bonnet, and would then ride behind him on the horse if she accepted him.

For the medicinal and domestic uses of some of these plants, see above in Chapter 2.

Bracken, Pteridium aquilinum; *d'la fouaille*, Fern.

A person wishing to win at cards gathered fern on St John's Day, and made a bracelet in the form of the letters **MUTY** with it. This was worn beneath the sleeve whilst playing. The letters had some cryptographic significance.

Elecampagne, Inula helenium; *iane dé campana*.

This was gathered on Midsummer Eve, and dried in an oven. It was then reduced to a powder, mixed with ambergris, and worn next to the heart for nine days. If you could then persuade the object of your desire to swallow a portion, they would love you.

On St. Thomas's Eve, if a girl stuck nine new pins in an onion, eight in a circle round a central pin, and placed it under her pillow, she would dream of her future husband. On the same night a girl might pass two new pins crosswise through a Golden Pippin apple (it had to be that variety), wrap it in the stocking taken from the left leg, and place it on the pillow. She then had to get into bed backwards, saying a long incantation to St. Thomas three times, and not utter another word. If she had performed the ceremony correctly, then her future husband would appear to her in a dream.

Yellow Horned-poppy, Glaucium flavum; *des jaunes pavots*.

The mediëval 'Ficus infernalis' was used by local witches in incantations.

Hemp, Cannabis sativa; *canivet*
To see a vision of her future husband, a girl must scatter hemp seed on the ground, say an incantation, and immediately run indoors. If she looks out she will then see her future husband mowing the hemp which will have grown mysteriously in a few minutes.

Agrimony, Agrimonia eupatoria; No Norman-French name found.
To dream of the man you will marry, place fronds of agrimony, each bearing nine leaflets under the pillow on St Thomas's Eve, and secure them with two crossed new pins.

Cannabis mas.
Male or Steele Hempe.

Roses, Rosa spp.; *Pied-de Chât* (The Sacred Briar).
A man afflicted with boils had to pass in silence, and fasting, under an arch of the plant on nine consecutive mornings, thus 'scraping off' the affliction. A similar cure was effected by passing under an arch of Bramble rooted at both ends.

Apple, Malus spp.; *la paomme*.
If one wished to know the initial of ones future spouse, it was necessary to peel an apple to make a continuous peeling, and throw this over the left shoulder. It would arrange itself on the ground in the initial of the future spouse's first name.
The punishment for stealing apples in Guernsey in 1611 was for the culprit to be *mis en collyere*, to have a wooden collar put round their neck.

Clovers, Trifolium spp.; *du traeffle*.
A four-leaved clover was a powerful love charm. It was placed on a consecrated stone, and Mass said over it. It was then incorporated into a nosegay given to the loved one. If they smelt the flowers, saying at the same time *Gabrielle ille sunt* they would return the love.
A four-leaved clover kept in ones boot brings good health, and a five-leaved one placed in the boot or shoe ensures continuing good luck.

Broom, Cytisus scoparius; *g'net* etc. (see above).
The witches 'broomstick' is known as a *genest* and was traditionally made from this plant, and was mounted at the chimney. Until the late 1980s, the Langfrie Hotel in Guernsey commemorated a traditional local coven

meeting place, with a life-size iron witch on a broomstick mounted on its chimney.

Gorse or **Furze**, Ulex europaeus; *du jaon*, and **Furze** or **Broom** (Cytisus scoparius; *bringe* or *g'nêt*) were, and still are placed in the chimneys of newly built premises by the builders to exclude evil spirits. The completion of the exterior construction of nearly all public or other important buildings in the islands is still celebrated with an official 'Topping-out ceremony'.

6. Local sayings about plants, or including plant names;

A *flleur de Mars - ni pouque, ni sac,*
A *flleur d'Avril - pougue et barris,*
A *flleur de Mai - barrique et tonne.*
'March blossom needs neither bag nor sack (for the fruit crop), April blossom fills bag and barrel, May blossom fills hogshead and tun'.

A *quand les sorchiers vaont au Catioroc i'passent pardessus bringe, bisaon, navire, et paissaon.* 'When the witches go to the Catioroc, they pass over broom, bramble, boat and fish'. (G).

I'faut d'la graisse pour la pllànte de cabboge; Il en faut étou a la cuire. 'Cabbage plants need fatness (manure), there must be fat to cook the cabbage too'.

Lé froment n'est pas l'valet de l'avogne. 'Wheat is not oat's servant'. (It must always be planted first).

I'faut souognier d'aver énne paömme pour la seit. One must keep an apple in store for the thirst. (Keep something in reserve).

Ne m'fait pas maönyair sus mon poummier d'suret. 'Do not make me climb my bitter apple-tree'. (Do not make me angry)

Nou' n'creit pas de preunes sus des poummiers. 'You can't expect plums to grow on apple trees'. (Don't expect the impossible).

La saërclle creit terjous. 'Weeds will always grow'.

Jaune coume q'zette, or *Jaonne coum du murlu* 'As yellow as a daffodil (or marigold)'.

Vert comme ache. 'As green as smallage'. (A herb allied to celery and parsley)

Noné n'est pas Noné sàns pâcrolle. 'Christmas is not Cristmas unless there be primroses'. *Pâcrolle, paquerelle,* (little plant of Easter) or *primevére,* were all used in Guernsey, and *pip'soles* in Jersey for Primroses.

Il vaut mûx pour ùn houme d'aver un percheux dans son ménage, qu'un frêne suis s'n héritage, 'It is better for a man to have a lazy man in his employ, than an ash tree on his estate'. It is believed that the shade of an ash tree is destructive to all vegetation beneath its spread, and to rob all nearby land of its goodness.

La cassidounne tout ma détrône 'Lavender heals all'.

Défaire énne touffe de persi, énne mort dans la famille 'To break up a parsley plant is to bring about a death in the family'.

+ 'Eate leekes with sorye [sorrel] in March, cresses in April, Ramsons [**Allium ursinum**, *l'ail des ours*] in May and all ye yeare after ye phisitions may goe play'.

Vert coum d'la chue. 'As green as chervil'. Used of someone with an unhealthy pallor.

7. Local Island names for Plants;

Many of these have medicinal or culinary uses which do not seem to differ from those which are recorded in England, and are therefore not separately described.

Seaweeds, referred to collectively as *Vraic or varech*, a few have their own names.

Kelp, Oarweed, or Tangleweeds, Laminaria spp.; *laminaire, chaudre dé vraic, des libaoux, du collet.*
Saw or Serrated Wrack, Fucus serratus; *vraic, vrec, varech, du cossard.*
Bladder Wrack, Fucus vesiculosus; *cossé du vraic, du gergeis.*
Sea bootlaces, Chorda filum; *llachets* (laces)
Carrageen, Chondrus crispus; *du carraguinne.*

Flowering Plants.
<u>Dicotyledons</u>
Larkspur, Consolida ajacis; *du pi d'alouaette* (G).
Traveller's-joy, Clematis vitalba; *d'la barbe d'vier bouonhomme* (Old-Man's-Beard) (J).
Meadow Buttercup, Ranunculus acris; *pid d'lliaön or pi de Yon* (lion's paw) *à rachaenes, boutaôn d'or, piépot* (fowl's-foot) (G), *du pipot* (J).
Creeping Buttercup, Ranunculus repens; *pid d'lliaôn lattai* (G), *du pipot* (J).
Bulbous Buttercup, Ranunculus bulbosus; *pid d'lliaôn à nouâle* (G), *du pipot* (J).
Lesser Spearwort, Ranunculus flammula; *faer dé lànce* (G), *des maillettes* (J).
Lesser Celandine, Ranunculus ficaria; *pissenlliet* (G), *du morrhouiton* (J).
Pheasant's-eye, Adonis annua; *goute dé sàng* (drop of blood) (G).
Columbine, Aquilegia vulgaris; *herbe d'lliaön, bounette* (G), *des vièrs garçons* (the old boys) (J).
Common Poppy, Papaver rhoeas; *coque, pavot sauvage, rose dé tchien* (G), *des roses à tchian* (Dog roses) (J).
Greater Celandine, Chelidonium majus; *d'l'hèrbe à véthues* (J). It is absent from the other islands.
Beech, Fagus sylvatica; *un fau* (J).

Sweet Chestnut, Castanea sativa; *Castanier, castognier* (G), *un chât'nyi* (J).
Silver Birch, Betula pendula; *un bouôlias* (J).
Good King Henry, Chenopodium bonus-henricus; *d's aulouoches* (J).
Many-seeded Goosefoot, Chenopodium polyspermum; *d'la rouoge s'nile* (J). (Red Goosefoot).
Stinking Goosefoot, Chenopodium vulvaria; *bllanche s'nile* (White Goosefoot) (G).
Nettle-leaved Goosefoot, Chenopodium murale; *d'la verte s'nile* (Green Goosefoot) (J).
Fat-hen, Chenopodium album; *snile, nère snile* (Black Goosefoot) (G), *d'la blianche s'nile* (White Goosefoot) (J).
Sea-beet, Beta vulgaris ssp. maritima; *bette d'banque* (G), *des bettes* (J).
Prickly Saltwort, Salsola kali; *du geon d'mielle* (dune gorse) (J).
Common Chickweed, Stellaria media; *moudräon, mourdron* (G), *du meurdron* (J). (Mouse's Eye).
Snow-in-Summer, Cerastium tomentosum; *d'l'argent* (Silver) (J).
Common Mouse-ear, Cerastium fontanum; *dé l'ouothelle dé souothis* (J).
Corn Spurrey, Spergula arvensis; *genouollère, genoillière* (G), *d'l'hèrbe à mille noeuds* (plant of a thousand nodes) (J).
Ragged-Robin, Lychnis flos-cuculi; *violette au vaër* (G), *du coucou d'pré* (J). (Meadow Cuckoo-flower).
Corncockle, Agrostemma githago; *Rose d'Tchen* (Dog-Rose) (G), *d'la nêle* (J)
Sea Campion, Silene maritima; *Eillet d'banque, eillet d'cauôte* (Seashore Pink) (G), *d's iliets d'rotchi, du blianc coucou, d'mouaîselles, blianches femmes, buonnefemmes* (J), the last three names coming from a child's game where the calyx is turned inside out and the petals removed to form a figure like a lady in a crinoline.
White Campion, Silene latifolia; *des vieil'yes fil'yes* (the spinsters) (J).
Red Campion, Silene dioica; *violette d'fossai, violette sauvage, violette à vée* (G), *d's iliets d'fossé* (J). (Bank violets).
Redshank, Polygonum maculosa, (P.persicaria); *courage, langue d'ouaie* (Goose-tongue), *herbe traitresse, rouge s'nile, rouge gàmbe* (G), *du paîvre à j'va* (Horse-pepper) (J).
Amphibious Bistort, Polygonum amphibia; *rouâge gambc, langue d'ouaie* (Goose-tongue), *herbe traitress* (G).
Water-pepper, Polygonum hydropiper; *du tcheurrhage* (J).
Knotgrass, Polygonum aviculare; *p'tite s'nile, d'la platte s'nile, s'nile nauetchie* (G), *d'la s'nile trainante* (Trailing Fathen) (J).
Buckwheat, Fagopyrum esculentum; *sarrâzin* (G).
Japanese Knotweed, Fallopia japonica; This Victorian garden import has

spread, and become naturalised in a number of places in Jersey (since 1915), Guernsey (since 1947), and Alderney (since about 1950). It is known locally as 'Donkey's Rhubarb'.
Black Bindweed, Fallopia convolvulus; *langue d'ouaie* (Goose-tongue), *vâle* (G), *du pèrsicarré* (J).
Sheep's Sorrel, Rumex acetosella; *p'tite surelle* (G), *d'la p'tite suthelle* (J).
Common Sorrel, Rumex acetosa; *surelle* (G), *d'la grande' suthelle*, *oseille* (J)
Wood Dock, Rumex sanguineus; *docque à sang* (G), *d'l'hèrbe à sang* (J).
Broad-leaved Dock, Rumex obtusifolius; *grande docque* (G), *des docques* (J).
Thrift, Armeria maritima; *eillet d'bànque. d'la g'laïe* (G).
Pansy, Viola tricolor; *pensée* (G).
Common Dog-violet, Viola riviniana; *coucou, pain d'coucou* (G).
White Poplar, Populus alba; *bian bouais* (G), *un blianc-bouais* (J).
Black Poplar, Populus nigra; *peupiller, peupier* (G).
Garlic Mustard, Alliaria petiolata; *d'la poummilière, poumilière* (G).
Wallflower, Erysimum cheiri; *violette d'châté* (Castle stock) (G), *d'la violette sauvage, ravenel* (J).
Virginia Stock, Malcolmia maritima; *du trichotin* (G).
Hoary Stock, Matthiola incana; *violette* (G).
Sea Stock, Matthiola sinuata; *d'la violette dé mielle* (Dune violet) (J). Only found in Jersey.
Water-cress, Rorippa nasturtium-aquaticum; *kerson* (G), *du cresson* (J).
Horse-radish, Armoracia rusticana; *d'la radiche à j'vaux* (J).
Cuckooflower, Cardamine pratensis; *jantchen, d'la pouôintcoute* (Whitsun Flower) (G), *du coucou* (J).
Sweet Alison, Lobularia maritima; *du riz* (Rice) (G), *d'l'alysson* (J).
Danish Scurvygrass, Cochlearia danica; *escorvie. C.* officinalis (Common Scurvygrass) is only found in Alderney.
Shepherd's-purse, Capsella bursa-pastoris; medicus, *pi d'mouissaon* (bird's foot), *p'tit c'psilaire* (G), *d'la bourse* (J)
Field Penny-cress, Thlaspi arvense; *monnoyère, moutardier* (G).
Swine-cress, Coronopus squamatus; *cône de cherf* (Stag's-horn) *kersounette* (G), *d'la cône dé chèr* (J).
Lesser Swine-cress, Coronopus didymus; *kersounette* (G), *du cresson à couochons* (J).
Rape, Brassica napus; *rabette* (G), *des suidiches* (J).
Turnip, Brassica rapa; *navet* (G), *des navets* (J).
Charlock, Sinapis arvensis; *berzac, beurza, poinfeis, d'la moutarde* (G), *du bréha* (J).
Sea Rocket, Cakile maritima; *la julienne.*
Sea-kale, Crambe maritima; *chou-mathin* (J).

Sea Radish, Raphanus raphanistrum ssp. maritimus; *d'la caboche sauvâge* (G), *du bréha* (J).
Weld, Reseda luteola; *garde, vaudre, herbe à toindre* (G), *d'l'hèrbe à teindre* (J).
Heather, Calluna vulgaris; *d'la bérouelle, brinche* (G), *d'la bruêthe* (J).
Cross-leaved Heath, Erica tetralix; *d'la bruëthe* (J)
Bell Heather, Erica cinerea; *béruelle, bervière* (G), *d'la bruêthe* (J).
Cowslip, Primula veris; *coucou* (G), *du jaune coucou* (J).
Primrose, Primula vulgaris; *paqu'rolles dé fossaï, paqu'rolles des courtis* (Easter flower, of bank or field) (G).
Scarlet Pimpernel, Anagallis arvensis; *pimpernelle* (G), *la baronmette ès pouôrres gens* (J) (Poor man's weather-glass).
Hydrangea, Hydrangea macrophylla; *du bott'ni beie* (Botany Bay, a local name widely used in Guernsey).
Red Currant, Ribes rubrum; *rouâges gradilles* (G), *des gradiles* (J).
Black Currant, Ribes nigrum; *nère gradille* (G). *des gradiles* (J).
Gooseberry, Ribes uva-crispa; *guerouaisier, queronaiseau* (G), *des grouaîsiles* (J).
English Stonecrop, Sedum anglicum; *pain d'souari* (Mouse's Bread) (G), *du pain à crapauds* (Toad's Bread) (J).
Silverweed, Potentilla anserina; *foûale à macré* (G), *d'la t'naisie* (J).
Wild Strawberry, Fragaria vesca; *frâses sauvage*.
Wood Avens, Geum urbanum; *d'l'hèrbe b'net* (J).
Dog Rose, Rosa canina; *Rose sauvage, rose dé cat, rose des fossais* (G).
Burnet Rose, Rosa pipinellifolia; *rose dé catte* (G).
Blackthorn, Prunus spinosa; *nère epäenne, nère epène, Mais d'Avril* (G), *d'la néthe êpîngne, eune preunelle* (J).
Dwarf Cherry, Prunus cerasus; *ch'lise, bayot* (G), *eune badgiole* (J).
Cherry Laurel, Prunus laurocerasus; *du louothie d'Espangne* (J).
Wild Pears, Pyrus spp.; *pairier* (G), *un paithyi sauvage* (J).
Crab Apple, Malus sylvestris; *paomme dé suret* (G).
Apple, Malus domestica; *poummier* (G), *un pommyi* (J).
Medlar, Mespilus germanica; *meslier, mêlier* (G), *un meîlyi* (J).
Common Bird's-foot-trefoil, Lotus corniculatus; *arrête-boeu, des p'tits chabots* (J).
Greater Bird's-foot-trefoil, Lotus pedunculatus; *grande rête-boeuf, träeffle d'iaou* (G).
Tufted Vetch, Vicia cracca; *hâzette* (G), *du véchon* (J).
Hairy Tare, Vicia hirsuta; *du véchon* (J).
Common Vetch, Vicia sativa; *vaëche* (G), *d'la vèche* (J).
Narrow-leaved Vetch, Vicia sativa ssp. nigra; *vicheron, vichon* (G).
Broad Bean, Vicia faba; *faïve* (G).

Restharrow, Ononis repens; *rête-boeuf* (G).
Ribbed Melilot, Melilotus officinalis; *du mélilot* (J).
Black Medick, Medicago lupulina; *du trêfl'ye à moutons* (J).
Lucerne, Medicago sativa; *luzerne* (G), *d'la lûzèrne* (J).
Sickle Medick, Medicago sativa ssp. falcata; *d'la luzerne* (G), *lûzèrne en faûil'ye* (J).
Spotted Medick, Medicago arabica; *du trêfl'ye d'Jérusalem* (J).
White Clover, Trifolium repens; *bllanc träeffle* (G), *du tréfl'ye d'natuthe* (J).
Slender Trefoil, Trifolium micranthum; *sain trèfle, sainsain, sainfouôin* (G).
Red Clover, Trifolium pratense; *grande träeffle* (G), *du rouoge tréfl'ye* (J).
Crimson Clover, Trifolium incarnatum; *incarnate* (G), *des soudards* (J), from the resemblance to the colour of the coats of the Jersey Militia.
Prostrate Broom, Cytisus scoparius ssp. maritimus; *du genêt d'falaise* (Cliff Broom) (J).
Gorse, Ulex europaeus; *du geon* etc.
Western Gorse, Ulex gallii; *d'la grappue* (J).
Spurge Laurel, Daphne laureola; *du sênné* (J).
Great Willowherb, Epilobium hirsutum; *violette d'Praï* (Meadow stock) (G).
Evening-primroses, Oenothera spp.; Known collectively as *des roses d'un jour*.
Fuchsia, Fuchsia magellanica; *patte-oreille* (Ear-rings) (G).
Box, Buxus sempervirens; *du buisse* (G).
Annual Mercury, Mercurialis annua; *fouarolle, fouirolle* (G), *d'la têtue* (J).
Petty Spurge, Euphorbia peplus; *lait d'souaris* (Mouse's milk), *herbe à verrue, fraincouaie, troupelâe* (G), *d'l'hèrbe ta véthues* (J).
Sun Spurge, Euphorbia helioscopia; *fouirolle* (G).
Flax, Linum usitatissimum; *Len* (G), *lin* (J), (Linseed).
Horse Chestnut, Aesculus hippocastaneum; *castongnia à poulôn* (G), *un chât'nyi à j'va* (J).
Wood-sorrel, Oxalis acetosella; *du pain coucou* (Cuckoo's bread), (J).
Oxalis, Oxalis spp. (O. corymbosa, O.latifolia, O.tetraphylla); known collectively as *du trêfl'ye ta ouognons*.
Herb-Robert, Geranium robertianum; *Rouâge gambe* (Red Leg) (G), *du rouoget* (J).
Garden Geraniums, Geranium spp.; *d'jerainiume* (G).
Common Stork's-bill, Erodium cicutarium; *des piègnes* (comb), from the beaks of the fruit looking like the teeth of a comb.
Nasturtium, Tropaeolum majus; *cupuchaon* (G).
Marsh Pennywort, Hydrocotyle vulgaris; *dôve* (G).
Sea Holly, Eryngium maritimum; *cardaön d'banque* (G), *du housse dé mielle* (J).

Alexanders, Smyrnium olusatrum; *Alisant* (G), *d'l'alisandre* (J).
Rock Samphire, Crithmum maritimum; *perchepierre, casse-pierre* (G), *d'la pèrche-pièrre* (J).
Fennel, Foeniculum vulgare; *fanoué* (G), *du fanon* (J).
Hemlock, Conium maculatum; *chue* (G), *d'la bênarde* (J).
Wild Celery, Apium graveolens; *du céléri sauvage*.
Fool's Watercress, Apium nodiflorum; *bêle*.
Hogweed, Heracleum sphondylium; known locally as Cow Parsnip, *quesse*.
Carrot, Daucus carota, D. carota ssp. maritima; *carotte* (G), *d'la cârotte sauvage* (J).
Common Centaury, Centaurium erythraea; *centurée, déblôimâie* (G), *d'l'hèrbe d'St Martin* (J).
Greater Periwinkle, Vinca major; *pervenche* (G), *d's êpèrvenches* (J).
Lesser Periwinkle, Vinca minor; *blluaette* (G).
Henbane, Hyocyamus niger; *hanebâne* (G), *d'la hannebanne* (J).
Deadly Nightshade, Atropa belladonna; *d'la chrysanthème au d'giâbl'ye* (J).
Bittersweet, Solanum dulcamara; *amerdou, amerdäon, morelle* (G), *d'l'amièrdoux* (J).
Field Bindweed, Convolvulus arvensis; *vâle, vaïle, pâlotte* (G), *des veil'yes dé r'lie* (J).
Sea Bindweed, Calystegia soldanella; *des veil'yes dé sablon* (J).
Hedge Bindweed, Calystegia sepium; *grande vâle, grande vaîle* (G), *des veil'yes* (J).
Bogbean, Menyanthes trifoliata; *faive de douit* (G), *du trêfl'ye dg'ieau* (J).
Purple Viper's-bugloss, Echium plantagineum; *d'la grâsse-g'linne* (J). Not found in the other islands.
Bugloss, Anchusa arvensis; *bourrage sauvage* (G), *d'la p'tite g'linne* (J).
Borage, Borago officinalis; *bourrage, bouarâge* (G), *du bouôrrage* (J).
Wood Forget-me-not, Myosotis sylvatica; *tricotin* (G), *des yeaux d'la Vierge* (the Virgin's Eyes) (J).
Tufted Forget-me-not, Myosotis laxa; *herbe d'azur* (G).
Early Forget-me-not, Myosotis ramosissima; *dé l'ouothelle dé souothis* (J).
Changing Forget-me-not, Myosotis discolor; *dé l'ouothelle dé souothis* (J).
Hedge Woundwort, Stachys sylvatica; *ortie puante* (Stinking Nettle) (G).
Marsh Woundwort, Stachys palustris; *coummaïre* (G), *d'l'orvale* (J).
Black Horehound, Ballota nigra; *du meuthe-en-c'mîn* (J).
Red Dead-nettle, Lamium purpureum; *rouâge ortie* (G), *d'l'enchens* (J).
Cut-leaved Dead-nettle, Lamium hybridum; *herbe au bourdon* (G).
Wood Sage, Teucrium scorodonia; *lambraise, ambrouaise* (G), *d'l'ambrais* (J).
Ground-ivy, Glechoma hederacea; *du tèrrêtre* (J).
Lilac, Syringa vulgaris; *lilas*.

Privet, Ligustrum vulgare; *d'la troène* (J).
Mulleins, Verbascum spp.; Collectively, *moleine* (G), *d'la molène* (J).
Snapdragon, Antirrhinum majus; *goule de lion* (G).
Common Toadflax, Linaria vulgaris; *bianche surelle* (G).
Thyme-leaved Speedwell, Veronica serpyllifolia; *veronique* (G).
Wall Speedwell, Veronica arvensis; *veronique.*
Ivy-leaved Speedwell, Veronica hederifolia; *herbe au bourdon* (Bee plant) (G), *du tèrrêtre* (J).
Yellow Rattle, Rhinanthus minor; *herbe à sonnettes, herbe ta sourettes* (G).
Bellflowers, Campanula spp.; *des cllochaettes* (G).
Sheep's-bit, Jasione montana; *eillet d'coti* (G), *des flieurs au dgiâbl'ye* (J).
Woodruff, Galium odoratum; *du ris* (J). The plant is not found in the other islands.
Lady's Bedstraw, Galium verum; *du myi d'mielle* (J).
Hedge Bedstraw, Galium mollugo; *contreprinse, pain de paenpaen* (G) (bread of the blood-nosed beetle, which eats the leaves).
Dwarf Elder, Sambucus ebulus; *yêble* (G).
Honeysuckle, Lonicera periclymenum; *suchets* (G), *du chuchet* (J) from *suchier,* to suck).
Red Valerian, Centranthus ruber; *du lilas d'Espangne* (J) (Spanish Lilies).
Wild Teasel, Dipsacus fullonum; *cardère, cardaon sauvage, cardère* (G), *du tcheurdron à chorchi* (J). Teasels are not common in the islands.
Burdocks, Arctium spp.; *boûillas* (G), *dé l'ouothelle d'âne* (J), where the fruits are known as *des prenants* or *des bouôlîns.*
Slender Thistle, Carduus tenuiflorus; known in Guernsey as the Seaside Thistle *cardaon d'bânque.*
Spear Thistle, Cirsium vulgare; *grand cardaon, cardaon béni, chardon béni* (G), *des soudards* (J).
Marsh Thistle, Cirsium palustre; *cardaon, mauvais chardon* (G), *tcheurdron* (J).
Creeping Thistle, Cirsium arvense; *petit cardaon, soudard, mauvais létron* (G), *du tcheurdron* (J).
Cornflower, Centaurea cyanus; *des bliuettes* (J).
This is rarely found in the other islands.
Rough Star-thistle, Centaurea aspera; *coultro* (J).
Chicory, Cichorium intybus; *chicorée* (G), *d'la chicorée sauvage* (J).
Cat's-ear, Hypochaeris radicata; *pllat laitraon* (flat sowthistle), *du pisse-en-lliet* (G).
Jersey Cudweed, Gnaphalium luteoalbum; *cottounière* (G).
Blue Fleabane, Erigeron acer; *d'l'herbe à puches* (J).
Confused Michaelmas-daisy, Aster novi-belgii; *la St. Michié* (G).
Mexican Fleabane, Erigeron karvinskianus; *des mèrgots à pouochins* (J).

Known throughout the islands as the 'St. Peter Port Daisy'.
Daisy, Bellis perennis; *berbiette* (Little Sheep) (G).
Tansy, Tanacetum vulgare; *tenaisie* (G), *d'la t'naisie* (J).
Sow-thistles, Sonchus spp.; known collectively as *laiträon* (G), *du laiteron* (J).
Dandelions, Taraxacum spp.; known collectively as *pllat laiträon* (G), *des pissenliets* (J). The fruits are known as *hôloges* (clocks).
Mugwort, Artemesia vulgaris; *l'herbe d'Saint Jean*. From its flowering at midsummer.
Wormwood, Artemesia absinthium; *iaune, alienne* (G), *d'l'absinthe* (J).
Sneezewort, Achillea ptarmica; *d's aigrettes* (J). It is rare in Alderney and not found in Guernsey, Sark or Herm.
Chamomile, Chamaemelum nobile; *auroque, d'la camière* (G).
Stinking Chamomile, Anthemis cotula; *méroque* (G).
Corn Marigold, Chrysanthemum segetum; *murlu* (G), *du mèneleu* (J).
Scented Mayweed, Matricaria recutita; *amroque* (G), *d'la m'soûque* (J).
Mayweeds, Tripleurospermum spp.; Collectively *d'la m'soûque* (J).
Ragwort, Senecio jacobea; *mèque* (G), *d's entaillies* (J).
Groundsel, Senecio vulgaris; *snichäon* (G), *du s'nichon* (J).
Heath Groundsel, Senecio sylvaticus; *du s'nichon* (J).
Marigold, Calendula officinalis; *sousique* (G), *d'la soucique* (J).
Soucique is derived from the latin 'solsequium' meaning a disc surrounded by rays, or a follower of the sun.

Monocotyledons;
Broad-leaved Pondweed, Potamogeton polygonifolius; *du vraic d'vivi* (J).
Curled Pondweed, Potamogeton crispus; *vraic du vivier* (Fishpond seaweed) (G).
Altar Lily, Zantedeschia aethiopica; *aireume* (G), generally known as the Arum Lily.
Common Duckweed, Lemna minor; *herbe à piraettes* (ducks) (G), *d'l'hèrbe d'pithot* (J).
Rushes, Juncus spp.; collectively known as *jonquet* a few species have their own names.
Sharp-flowered Rush, Juncus acutiflorus; *joncree* (G).
Toad Rush, J. bufonius; *saie de Trie* (G).
Soft Rush, J. effusus; *jonc or joncre* (G).
Field Woodrush, Luzula campestris; *pi d'alouette* (Lark's foot), (G). This is known in the islands as **Good Friday** Grass because it will always be found in flower on that day.

Great Fen-sedge, Cladium mariscus; *du pavis* (J). This species does not occur in the other islands.
Sheep's-fescue, Festuca ovina; *herbe à moutons.*
Perennial Rye-grass, Lolium perenne; *raie-grasse* (G), *d'l'hèrbe pèrpétuelle* (J).
Italian Rye-grass, Lolium multiflorum; *d'l'hèrbe italienne* (J).
Quaking-grass, Briza media; *herbe trembllànte, herbe dé Jacob,* (G).
Greater Quaking-grass, Briza maxima; *des lèrmes d'Jâcob* (J). Rarely found in the other islands.
Annual Meadow-grass, Poa annua; *d'l'hèrbe à poules* (J).
Smooth Meadow-grass, Poa pratensis; *d'l'hèrbe d'pré* (J).
Cock's-foot, Dactylis glomerata; *du pid-d'co* (J).
False Oat-grass, Arrhenatherum elatius; *tchendent* (Dog's-tooth) (G).
Wild Oat, Avena fatua; *avenon* (G).
Yorkshire Fog, etc, Holcus spp.; *molle hèrbe.*
Silver Hair-grass, Aira caryophyllea; *d'la finne hèrbe* (J).
Early Hair-grass, Aira praecox; *du suthin* (J).
Sweet Vernal Grass, Anthoxanthum odoratum; *du tchiândent* (J).
Creeping Bent, Agrostis stolonifera; *du traïnaïn, trainaon, bllue herbe* (G).
Hare's-tail, Lagurus ovatus; *poussé dé bànque* (G), *des babinnes-dé-lièvre* (J).
Marsh Foxtail, Alopecurus geniculatus; *herbe pointue* (G).
Timothy, Phleum pratense; *d'la coue* (J).
Bromes, Bromus spp.; collectively known as *droe.*
Couch-grasses, Elymus spp,; collectively known as *bâs* (G), *du bas* (J).
Wall Barley, Hordeum murinum; *herbe sorchière* (G), *du blie sauvage* (J).
Cockspur, Echinochloa crusgalli; *d'l'hèrbe à pithot, d'la canârie* (J).
Hairy Finger-grass, Digitaria sanguinalis; *du pid-d'alouette* (Lark's-foot) (J).
Bulrush, Typha latifolia; *pavie* (G).

Bulbous plants
Orange Day-lily, Hemerocallis fulva; *liss-d'aen-jour* (One-day lily) (G).
Lily-of-the-valley, Convallaria majalis; *du mudget* (G).
Star-of-Bethlehem, Ornithogallum umbellatum; *d's êtailes dé Bethléem* (J).
Bluebell, Hyacinthoides non-scripta; *côneille* (G), *des clioches dé Carême* (J).
Neapolitan Garlic, Allium neapolitanum; *la Betléhem* (G). Known in Guernsey as **Guernsey Star of Bethlehem**.
Round-headed Leek, Allium sphaerocephalon; *des gênottes* (J).
Crow Garlic, Allium vineale; *d'l'ail sauvage* (J).
Ramsons, Allium ursinum; *l'ail des ours* (J).

Snowdrop, Galanthus nivalis; *des bouonnefemmes* (J).
Jonquils, Narcissus x spp.; *qu'saette* (G).

Butcher's-broom, Ruscus aculeatus; *prunet, vaërt, vaer genêt, du brousse* (G), *du frêgon* (J).
Stinking Iris, Iris foetidissima; *gliei* (G).
Sand Crocus, Romulea columnae; *génotte* (G), *des genottes* (J), (earthnut).
Eastern Gladiolus, Gladiolus communis; *d's êtchelles dé Jâcob* (Jacob's ladder) (J).
Montbretia, Crocosmia x crocosmiflora; *étchelles* (ladders) (G).
Black Bryony, Tamus communis; *briaonne* (G).
Heath Spotted-orchid, Dactylorhiza maculata; *d'la coue dé r'nard* (fox's tail) (J).
Loose-flowered Orchid, Orchis laxiflora; *pennecoûte* (G), *des pentecôtes* (J). Locally common in Guernsey and Jersey, and absent from Alderney, Sark, and Herm. It flowers at Pentecost. It is known in Jersey as the 'Jersey Orchid'.
Early Purple Orchid, Orchis mascula; *pain de couleuvre* (Adder's bread) (G). This is a strange name, probably imported from Normandy, since there are no snakes in Guernsey, and the orchid is rare in both Guernsey and Jersey, and absent from the other islands.

BIBLIOGRAPHY

Anstead, D.T. & Latham R.G	*The Channel Islands*	1862
Bonnard, B.	*Flora of Alderney; a Checklist with Notes*	1988
Closs, Amanda	*Tastes of the Channel Islands*	1983
Cook, Doris C.	*An Elizabethan Guernseyman's MS Book. Published in The Channel Islands Annual Anthology 1972-3*	1972
de Garis, Marie	*Dictiounnaire Angllais-Guernesiais. 3rd Ed.*	1982
	Folklore of Guernsey	1975
La Société Guernesiaise	*Transactions*	1882-1992
La Société Jersiaise	*Bulletin*	1873-1991
Le Sueur, Frances	*Flora of Jersey*	1984
McClintock, D.	*The Wild Flowers of Guernsey*	1974
MacCulloch, Sir E.	*Guernsey Folklore*	1903
Marquand, E.D.	*Flora of Guernsey & the Lesser Channel Islands*	1901
Métivier, G.	*Dictionnaire Franco-Normand*	1870
Stevens, C. Arthur J. & Stevens, A.	*Jersey Place Names*	1986

ACKNOWLEDGEMENTS

The works mentioned in the bibliography have all proved helpful in researching this volume. In addition I should like to express my special thanks to Doris Cook for her kind permission to use the manuscript of her translation/transcription of the Elizabethan Guernseyman's MS Book; also to the Librarians of the Priaulx Library in Guernsey and La Société Jersiaise for giving help and access to their collections. Scraps of material have been gleaned over several years reading, from the an nual volumes of La Société Guernesiaise *Transactions* and La Société Jersiaise *Bulletin*, both covering more than a century.

The woodcut illustrations have all been taken from Thomas Johnson's 1633 edition of John Gerard's *The Herbal or General History of plants* first published in 1597.

Index

A

Adder's bread, 64
Agrimony, 23, 42, 52
Alderney Thorn, 27
Alderney Week, 44
Alexanders, 59
Alison, Sweet, 57
Andros, Thomas, 10, 30
Angelica, 27
Apple, 3, 23, 41, 49, 52, 54, 58
    Crab, 58
    Golden Pippin, 51
Ash, 3, 31, 54

B

Balm, 29
Barley, Wall, 63
Basil, 29
Bay, 13, 39
Bear's-foot, 5
Bedstraw, 61
Bedstraw, Lady's, 61
Beech, 55
Beet, 16
Bellflower, 61
Betony, 42
Bindweed, Black, 57
    Field, 60
    Hedge, 60
    Sea, 60
Bird's-foot-trefoil,
    Common, 58
    Greater, 58
Bistort, Amphibious, 56
Bittersweet, 60
Black Butter, 42, 49
Blackberry, 3, 21
Blackthorn, 23, 41, 58
Bladderwrack, 11
Bluebell, 63
    White, 37
Bogbean, 60
Borage, 28, 60
Box, 59
Bracken, 3, 12, 51
Bramble, 21, 52
Branchage, Le, 43
Brandons, Les, 44
BrÉvint, Rev. Elie, 35
Broad Bean, 58
Broken-heart, 27
Brome grasses, 63
Brooklime, 32
Broom, 3, 24, 42, 52
    Prostrate, 59
Bryony, Black, 64
Buckwheat, 56
Bugloss, 28, 60
Bulrush, 63
Burdock, 61
Butcher's-broom, 64
Buttercup, 13
    Bulbous, 55
    Creeping, 55
    Goldilocks, 13
    Meadow, 55

C

Cabbage, 54
    Giant, 19
    Jersey, 41
Campion, Red, 56
    Sea, 56
    White, 56
Carpenter's plant, 35
Carrageen, 11, 55
Carrot, 27, 60
Castle stock, 57
Cat's-ear, 61
Catch the Devil, 40
Celandine, Greater, 26, 55
    Lesser, 40, 55
Celery, Wild, 60
Centaury, Common, 60
Chamomile, 62
    Stinking, 62
Charlock, 49, 57
Cherry, Dwarf, 58
Cherry Laurel, 58
Chervil, 54
    Garden, 26
Chestnut, Sweet, 56
    Horse, 59
Chickweed, Common, 56
Chicory, 61
Christmas Rose, 5
Cider, 50
Clary, 6
    Wild, 31
Cleavers, 43
Cliff Broom, 59
Clover, 52
    Crimson, 59
    Red, 59
    White, 59
Cock's-foot, 63
Cockspur, 63
Coltsfoot, 35
Columbine, 55
Comfrey, 4, 7, 28
    Russian, 7, 28
Corncockle, 56
Cornflower, 61
Cornsalad, 32
Couch, Common, 37
Couch-grasses, 63
Cowslip, 19, 58
Creeping Bent, 63
Crocus, Sand, 64
Cuckooflower, 57
Cudweed, 33
    Jersey, 61
Currant, Black, 58
    Red, 58

D

Daisy, 62
    Oxeye, 35
    St. Peter Port, 61
Dandelion, 33, 49, 62
Dead-nettle, Cut-leaved, 60
    Red, 60
Devil's apples, 28
Devil's grapes, 27
Dock, 49
    Broad-leaved, 57
    Wood, 57
Dodder, 28
Dog-violet, 57
Donkey's Rhubarb, 57
Dropwort, 20
Duckweed, 62
Duke of Argyll's Teaplant, 27
Dune Gorse, 56

E

Eel-grass, 36
Elder, 3, 32, 42
    Dwarf, 61
Elecampagne, 29, 34, 51
Elm, 3
Evening-primrose, 59
Eyebright, 32

Index

F

Fat-hen, 56
Fennel, 26, 60
Ferns, 12
Feverfew, 34
Fig, 3, 14
Figwort, Common, 31
Flax, 3, 59
Fleabane, 34
    Blue, 61
    Mexican, 61
Flowering Plants, 13, 55
Forget-me-not, Changing, 60
    Early, 60
    Tufted, 60
    Wood, 60
Forthe, Doris, 10
Foxglove, 31
Foxtail, Marsh, 63
Fuchsia, 59
Fumitory, 40
Furze, 3, 53

G

Galingale, 36
Garlic, 38
    Crow, 63
    Neapolitan, 63
    Three-cornered, 37
    Wild, 37, 49
Garlic Mustard, 57
Garnesee Violets, 19
Geranium, Garden, 59
Gladiolus, Eastern, 64
Good Friday Grass, 62
Good King Henry, 56
Goose-tongue, 56
Gooseberry, 58
Goosefoot, Many-seeded, 56
    Nettle-leaved, 56
    Stinking, 56
Gorse, 53, 59
    Western, 59
Gosselin, Joshua, 18
Great Fen-sedge, 62
Great Ploughing, The, 43
Green bed, 12, 36, 51
Ground-ivy, 60
Groundsel, 35, 62
    Heath, 62

H

Hair-grass, Early, 63
    Silver, 63
Hairy Finger-grass, 63
Hare's-tail, 63
Harvest Customs, 47
Hawthorn, 23, 41
Hazel, 3, 16
Heath, Cross-leaved, 58
Heather, 3, 58
    Bell, 58
Hellebore, 4, 5, 13
    Black, 5
    Green, 5
    Stinking, 5
Helleborine, White False, 5
Hemlock, 60
Hemlock Water Dropwort, 42, 49
Hemp, 3, 14, 52
Hemp-Agrimony, 36
Henbane, 60
Herb-Robert, 59
Herb of Gladness, 28
Herb of Grace, 7
Hogweed, 27, 49, 60
Holly, Sea, 59
Holy Herb, 9
Honeysuckle, 61
Hop, 3
Horehound, Black, 60
    White, 29
Horse-pepper, 56
Horse-radish, 57
Houseleek, 19, 29
Hydrangea, 58

I

Iris, Stinking, 64
    Yellow, 39
Ivy, 26

J

Jonquils, 64
Jour des Vitres, Le, 44
Jove's Beard, 19
Juno's Tears, 9

K

Kelp, 55
King of the Woods, 41
Knapweed, Common, 32
Knotgrass, 56
Knotweed, Japanese, 56
Knowleton, Thomas, 39

L

Lady's plant, 31
Larkspur, 55
Lavender, 4, 5, 30, 39, 54
Laver Bread, 11
Le Mesurier, Governor John, 48
Leek, 39
    Round-headed, 63
Lent lilies, 39
Lilac, 60
Lily, Guernsey, 39
    Jersey, 39
    Madonna, 39
    Altar, 62
Lily-of-the-Valley, 39, 63
Lingwort, 5
Local Names, 55
Local sayings, 54
Long Jack, 19, 41
Lords-and-Ladies, 36
Love-lies-Bleeding, 16
Love Charms, 51
Lucerne, 59
Lupin, Tree, 24
Lyte's Herbal, 19

M

Magic Uses, 51
Mallow, Common, 18
Marigold, 35, 62
    Corn, 62
Marjoram, 4, 8, 39
    Pot, 8, 29
    Sweet, 8
    Wild, 29
Marram, 37
Mauvaises Herbes Laws, 48
May-day, 44
Mayweeds, 62
Meadow-grass, Annual, 63
    Smooth, 63

Index

Meadow Cuckoo-flower, 56
Medick, Black, 59
    Sickle, 59
    Spotted, 59
Medlar, 58
Melilot, Ribbed, 59
Mercury, Annual, 59
Mercury's Moist Blood, 9
Michaelmas-daisy, Confused, 61
Midsummer Eve, 51
Milk-a-Punch, 45
Milk-a-Punch Sunday, 45
Milkwort, 21, 25
Mint, Garden, 30
Montbretia, 64
Mother of Thyme, 30
Motherwort, 29
Mouse-ear, Common, 56
Mouse's Bread, 58
Mouse's Eye, 56
Mugwort, 62
Mullein, 61
    Black, 31
    Great, 31
Mustard, Garlic, 57
    Hedge, 18, 49

N

Narcissus, 39
Nasturtium, 59
Navelwort, 19
Neesewort, 5
Neesingroot, 5
Nettle, 15, 49
Nightshade, Black, 27
    Deadly, 60
Nine Healing Herbs, 4, 25, 30, 34

O

Oak, 3, 40
Oarweed, 55
Oat, 54
    Wild, 63
Oat-grass, False, 63
Oats, 37
Onion, 37
Onions, Stinking, 49
Orange Day-lily, 63
Orchid, Early Purple, 64

Orchid, Heath Spotted-, 64
    Jersey, 64
    Loose-flowered, 64
Oregano, 8
Osier, 18
Oxalis, 59

P

Pansy, 57
Parsley, 26, 54
    Fool's, 42
Parsnip, 43
    Cow, 49
    Water, 34
Pea-haulms, 12
Peach, 3
Pear, Wild, 58
Pellitory-of-the-Wall, 16
Penny-cress, Field, 57
Pennywort, Marsh, 59
Peony, 17
Periwinkle, Greater, 60
    Lesser, 60
Pheasant's-eye, 55
Plantain, Ribwort, 31
Pondweed, Broad-leaved, 62
    Curled, 62
Poplar, Black, 57
    White, 57
Poppy, 40, 55
Pot Pourri, 39
Potato, 27
Primrose, 54, 58
Privet, 60
Purple Moor-grass, 37
Purslane, Common, 17

Q

Quaking-grass, 63
    Greater, 63
Quinces, 23

R

Radish, Sea, 57
Ragged-Robin, 56
Ragwort, 49, 62
Ramsons, 63
Rape, 57
Red Leg, 59
Redshank, 40, 56

Reed, 3
    Common, 37
Restharrow, 58
    Common, 23
Rocket, Sea, 57
Rose, 41, 52
    Burnet, 58
    Dog, 40, 58
Rosemary, 4, 6, 30, 39, 42
Rue, 4, 7, 25
    Meadow, 7
Rush, 3, 12, 62
    Compact, 36
    Sharp-flowered, 62
    Soft, 36, 62
    Toad, 62
Rye-grass, Italian, 63
    Perennial, 63

S

Sacred Briar, 52
Saffron, 3
Sage, 4, 6, 30
Saltwort, 35
    Prickly, 56
Samphire, Rock, 26, 60
Saxifrage, 20
Scarlet Pimpernel, 58
Scurvygrass, Common, 57
    Danish, 57
Sea-beet, 56
Sea-kale, 57
Sea bootlaces, 55
Sea Holly, 59
Sea Lettuce, 11
Sea Radish, 57
Sea Rocket, 57
Seashore Pink, 56
Seaweeds, 11, 55
Sedge, 3
Setter-wort, 5
Sheep's-bit, 61
Sheep's-fescue, 63
Shepherd's-purse, 57
Silver Birch, 56
Silverweed, 58
Small Sage, 31
Smallage, 54
Snapdragon, 61
Sneezewort, 62
Snow-in-Summer, 56
Snowdrop, 63

Index

Soapwort, 17
Sorrel, Common, 57
   Sheep's, 57
Sow-thistles, 62
Sowing seeds, 49
Sowthistle, Flat, 61
Spearwort, Lesser, 13, 55
Speedwell, Germander, 32
   Ivy-leaved, 61
   Thyme-leaved, 61
   Wall, 61
Spleenwort, Black, 12
Spring Juyce, 32
Spurge, Caper, 25
   Petty, 59
   Sun, 25, 59
Spurge Laurel, 59
Spurrey, Corn, 56
Squinancywort, 25
St. John's-wort, 17
   Perforate, 40
St. John's Eve, 51
St. Thomas's Eve, 51
Star-of-Bethlehem, 63
Star-thistle, Rough, 61
Star of Bethlehem, Guernsey, 63
Stock, Castle, 57
   Hoary, 19, 57
   Sea, 57
   Virginia, 57
Stonecrop, Biting, 20
   English, 58
   Large Yellow, 20
Stop-ox, 23
Stork's-bill, Common, 59
   Musk, 26
Strawberry, 23
Strawberry, Wild, 58
Swine-cress, 57
   Lesser, 57

T

Tamarisk, 18
Tangleweed, 55
Tare, Hairy, 58
Teasel, Wild, 61
Thistle, 3
   Creeping, 49, 61
   Marsh, 49, 61
   Seaside, 61
   Slender, 61

Thistle, Smooth Sow-, 33
   Spear, 32, 49, 61
Thorn, 3
Thorn-apple, 28
Thrift, 57
Thyme, 29, 39
   Wild, 30
Timothy, 63
Toad's Bread, 58
Toadflax, Common, 61
Topping-out, 53
Tormentil, 21, 25
Traveller's-joy, 55
Trefoil, Slender, 59
Turnip, 57
Tutsan, 17

V

Valerian, Red, 61
Venus' Navel-wort, 19
Vervain, 4, 9, 28
Vetch, Common, 58
   Kidney, 23
   Narrow-leaved, 58
   Tufted, 58
Viper's-bugloss Purple, 60
Vraic, 45, 55

W

Wallflower, 57
Walnut, 3
Water-cress, 57
Water-lily, White, 13
Water-pepper, 56
Watercress, Fool's, 60
Weld, 58
Wheat, 54
Whitethorn, 41
Whitsun Flower, 57
Willow, 3
Willowherb, Great, 59
Winter Heliotrope, 35
Wood-sorrel, 59
Wood Avens, 58
Wood Sage, 60
Woodruff, 61
Woodrush, Field, 62
Wormwood, 4, 8, 34, 62
Woundwort, Hedge, 60
   Marsh, 60
Wrack, Bladder, 55
   Serrated, 55

Y

Yarrow, 34
Yellow Horned-poppy, 51
Yellow Rattle, 61
Yellow Toad's-bread, 20
Yew, 3
Yorkshire Fog, 63